Berlin Tomorrow

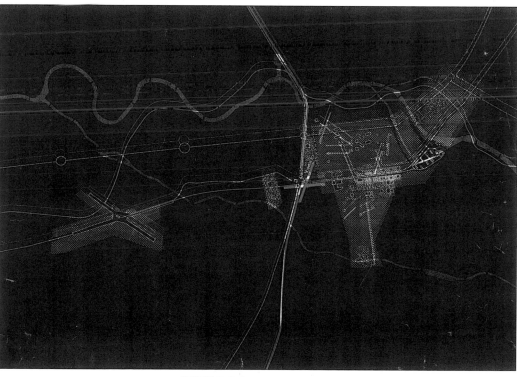

COOP HIMMELBLAU, 'CROSSING POINTS'

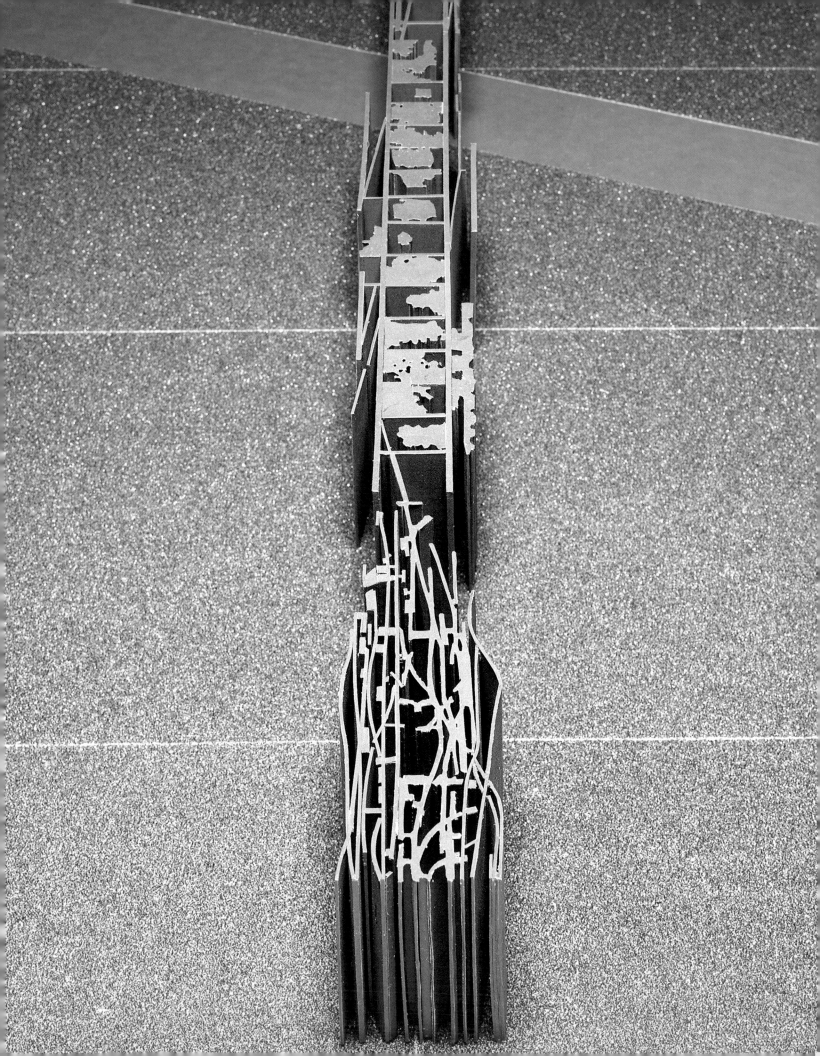

Architectural Design
Edited by Andreas C Papadakis

Berlin Tomorrow

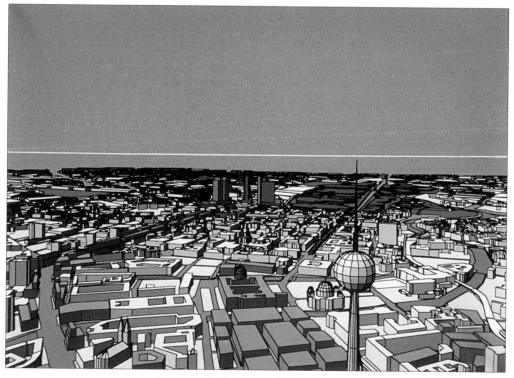

OPPOSITE: DANIEL LIBESKIND, 'ÜBER DEN LINDEN'
ABOVE: HANS KOLLHOFF, 'CITY LIMITS'

ACADEMY EDITIONS · LONDON

Acknowledgements

...cture Museum in Frankfurt and especially director Vittorio
...llaboration on this issue. This is the third time that *Architec-
tural Design* magazine has taken Berlin as a subject of study. Each time discovering a new facet, on
this occasion we look at the future of Berlin and the incredible opportunities which it holds.

The articles *An Exhibition of Pictures* (*pp 8-10*), *Ideas for the Heart of A Great City* (*pp 12-15*) and
Growing Together Again (*pp 16-19*) were translated from the German by Eileen Martin

Photographs

Most of the photographs are supplied by the German Architecture Museum, Frankfurt. We are also
grateful to the architects who provided material, and at such short notice. Credits are as follows:
pp 25, 28-29 Dieter Leistner; *pp 64-69* Udo Hesse

EDITOR
Dr Andreas C Papadakis

EDITORIAL OFFICES: 42 LEINSTER GARDENS, LONDON W2 3AN TELEPHONE: 071-402 2141
CONSULTANTS: Catherine Cooke, Dennis Crompton, Terry Farrell, Kenneth Frampton, Charles Jencks
Heinrich Klotz, Leon Krier, Robert Maxwell, Demetri Porphyrios, Colin Rowe, Derek Walker
EDITORIAL TEAM: Maggie Toy (House Editor), James Steele (Senior Editor), Vivian Constantinopoulos, Nicola Hodges
DESIGNED BY: Andrea Bettella, Mario Bettella SUBSCRIPTIONS MANAGER: Mira Joka

First published in Great Britain in 1991 by *Architectural Design*
an imprint of the
ACADEMY GROUP LTD, 7 HOLLAND STREET, LONDON W8 4NA
ISBN: 1-85490-104-4 (UK)

Architectural Design Profile 92 is published as part of *Architectural Design* Vol 61 7-8 /1991
Published in the United States of America by
ST MARTIN'S PRESS, 175 FIFTH AVENUE, NEW YORK 10010
ISBN: 0-312-06783-6 (USA)

Printed and bound in Singapore

Contents

ARCHITECTURAL DESIGN PROFILE No.92

Berlin Tomorrow

Guest Edited by Vittorio Magnago Lampugnani

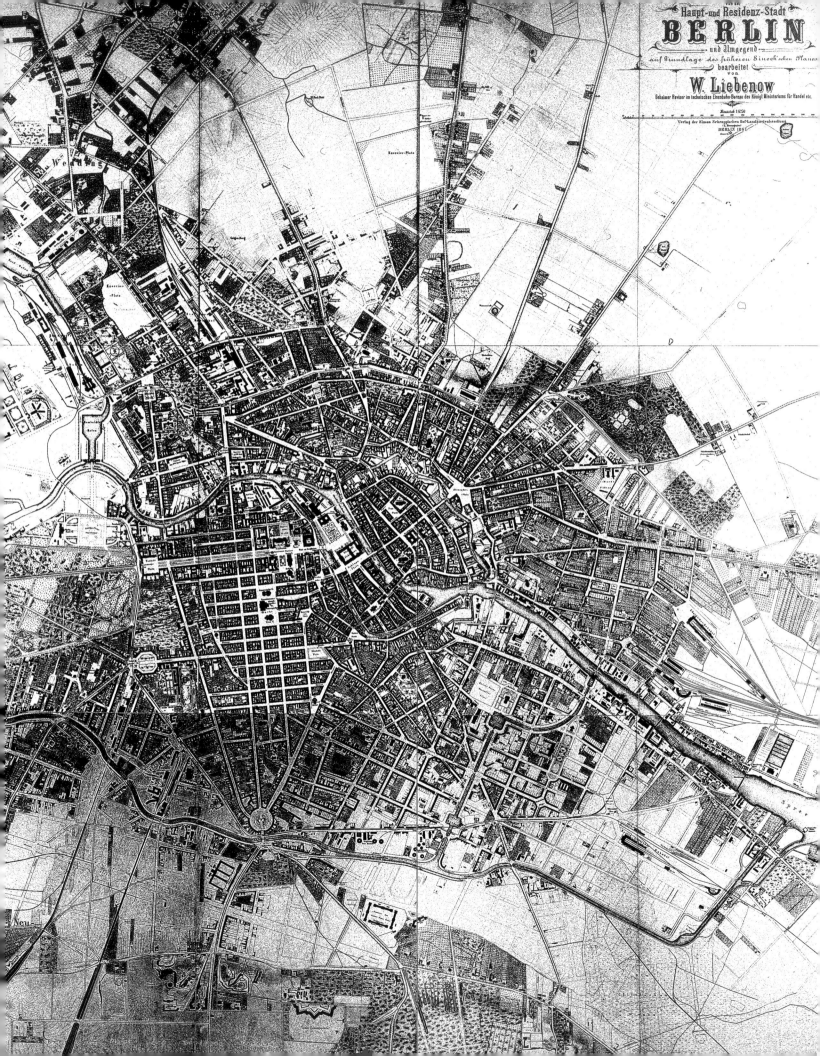

von der
Haupt- und Residenz-Stadt
BERLIN
und Umgegend
auf Grundlage des früheren Sineck'schen Planes
bearbeitet
von
W. Liebenow
Geheimer Revisor im technischen Eisenbahn-Bureau des Königl. Ministeriums für Handel etc.

Maasstab 1:650

Verlag der Simon Schropp'schen Hof-Landkartenhandlung
BERLIN 1857.

KENNETH POWELL
BERLIN – CITY OF THE FUTURE

Adolf Hitler imagined a Berlin 'built on such a scale that St Peter's and its Square will seem like toys in comparison'. 'Nothing', declared Hitler, 'will be too good for the beautification of Berlin'. His dream ended in 1945, when Berlin became a modern Carthage. Some argued that the city should be left in this state: a monument to defeat. But Berlin survived the Allied bombs and nearly half a century of division; and now, new architectural visions are dreamt.

The scramble is on to rebuild Berlin – but as what? The capital of the reunited Germany? German reunification has taken place at a time when the nation state is in decline in Europe. Berlin's ambitions are and must be to emerge as a great European metropolis. In some ways it has never been this in all its history. Berlin is Europe's ultimate city of the future – if only because so much of its past is too painful to contemplate – and where the historically informed urbanism of today grapples with the elusive identity of a city which does not know its own identity.

Writing of Berlin nearly a decade ago Leon Krier insisted 'modern architecture and town planning are incapable of creating localities of human dignity. The exhibition 'Berlin Tomorrow' attempted to prove Krier wrong: to present a series of visions which are concerned with creating dignified and humane places. Only a few years ago, this seemed to be the mission of the IBA – yet the philosophy of the latter was essentially, maybe inevitably, escapist, an *ad hoc* Post-Modern response to disorder. Now the new European architecture moves centre-stage in a dramatic bid to resolve the contradictions of the city.

The heart of the city is, in effect, up for grabs. The Potsdamerplatz – the real, if never the formal, heart of Berlin – has been largely bought up by Daimler Benz. Fears that the transaction is the beginning of a development scramble have not been altogether stilled by the appointment of Richard Rogers as master-planner. Lampugnani insists that the aim of 'Berlin Tomorrow' was neither visionary nor critical but practical – an intervention in the replanning process and an attempt to present alternatives to the opportunism of the developers.

Nostalgia in Berlin is a dangerous business – nostalgia for what, and for when? Presumably for the Berlin of the 1920s and early 30s, the Berlin of Weil, Brecht and Lenya. How can the culture of Berlin in the one era when it was indubitably a world city be encapsulated in architecture when the regime that swept it all away was obsessed with architectural aggrandisement? Follow this line of argument through and you come to the most obvious argument for a Deconstructivist Berlin. Daniel Libeskind takes this exploration of the spirit of the city to heart and tries to release the energies he sees pent-up by formal planning providing a slap in the face for the smug politeness of the IBA. However, Libeskind is no architectural hooligan, nor is he indulging in Archigram-style flights of fancy. His proposal is representative of a concern for rooting architecture in a social ethos.

OM Ungers wants to provide Berlin with its own ready-made collection of Modern monuments by building unbuilt projects by Mies, Adolf Loos, Lissitzky and others. This retrospective monumentalism is a logical corollary of Ungers' view of Berlin as urban chaos. For him, Berlin needs to be subjected to a strict audit, with parts of the city that fail to measure up to future needs radically recast or even razed.

Modernist monumental ambitions lie at the heart of 'Berlin Tomorrow'. In Berlin the associations of monumentalism are unfortunate – Albert Speer and the Stalinist megalomania of the 1950's GDR. Scharoun's Kultur Forum represents a Modernism that is anti-monumental, even anti-place. Buildings drift randomly in a formless cityscape – chaos and destruction are celebrated rather than acknowledged.

The participants in 'Berlin Tomorrow' were confronted by a city in the process of transformation – as the case of the Potsdamerplatz confirms, the process is underway. The city authorities are already besieged, it seems, by planning applications. Few of them are concerned with 'the spirit of the city', which Libeskind urges architects and planners to probe. The exhibition therefore becomes a concerted campaign to hold back the tide and lay down the ground rules for sane development.

Berlin, says Michael Mönninger, is an ugly city, whose ugliness, however, is a symbol of freedom. It has the chance to become the representative urban form of the late 20th century – free and yet beautiful, ordered yet permissive. It is this vision which the exhibition, and this issue which celebrates it, explores. Berlin is not the only great European city to contemplate radical changes in preparation for the urban horse-race of the next decade or so. In Paris, new quarters and new monuments are the result of political direction from the centre – from the Mairie de Paris and the Elysée. In London, restructuring mirrors a *laissez-faire* philosophy, the drawbacks of which are becoming more apparent by the day. Can Berlin, with its rich but tragic history, avoid excesses of order and licence?

The central issue is: what sort of a new heart should Berlin be given? Wary of urban antipathy, JP Kleihues proposes a great mass of buildings, including Chicago-style towers. Giorgio Grassi counterpoises urban regularity with open parkland. The Wall cannot disappear from memory as easily as it has vanished from the face of the city. But the task of uniting East and West remains. Mirroring, perhaps, the fears and suspicions, as well as the hopes and aspirations, of contemporary Berliners, Bernard Tschumi treats the great historic divide as a kind of river to be bridged over. The vacuum at the city's core becomes the generator of its renaissance. Where there was once the Piccadilly Circus of Germany and then the GDR's killing-ground Tschumi proposes an arena for celebrations, demonstrations, circuses and gatherings. The reordered centre of Berlin thus becomes the embodiment of freedom. History is vindicated.

Plan of Berlin by W Liebenow, 1867

Kenneth Powell is Correspondent for The Daily Telegraph, *and member of the Academy Forum Council*

VITTORIO MAGNAGO LAMPUGNANI
AN EXHIBITION OF PICTURES

The exhibition documented in this issue is an exhibition of pictures. Pictures of how 17 international architects want to see the future centre of Berlin.

Pictures are appealing. One can imagine what they show, one can think it is good or bad, one can discuss it. This is what we wanted – a broad, controversial and fruitful discussion on the future architectural and urban planning of Berlin. That is why we invited the architects to conjure up pictures. But pictures can also be confusing, they suggest that what they show is meant literally, intended to be definitive and that is just what we did not want – ultimate plans for the future architecture of Berlin, an attempt to fix the planning once and for all. It was just what the architects did not want and could not do. But they have repeatedly been judged by this criterion, and probably always will be. That is the advantage and disadvantage of pictures: one needs them to have a public discussion on real future perspectives, but once they exist they suggest the end point of a discussion which they were only intended to start. It is also the advantage and disadvantage of this exhibition. In order to achieve its objective (namely, discussion), it had to risk being taken for something it did not want to be: a presentation of plans for Berlin.

But that is to anticipate. First I believe I should give a brief report. If I were asked to date the birth of the project which is the subject of this issue, I would say it was an evening in October last year, when Michael Mönninger, Mathias Schreiber and I had a meal together. As we talked, the project 'Berlin Tomorrow: Ideas for the Heart of a Great City' began to take shape. We believed the best architects all over the world should be asked to develop ideas for a possible rearrangement of the historical centre of Berlin, which suddenly became possible when the Wall came down. These ideas (it would be too much to say designs) should be shown to as broad a public as possible, both by being published in the *Frankfurter Allgemeine Zeitung* and through an exhibition at the German Architecture Museum. For the latter, an extensive catalogue would of course be published. That evening we only discussed the rudimentary outline of all this. How could it have been otherwise? The director and publisher of the *Frankfurter Allgemeine Zeitung* had not even been asked whether they would agree to such an action, quite unusual for a daily paper and the German Architecture Museum, which is, after all, in Frankfurt and not in Berlin, had neither the mandate nor the funds for such an undertaking.

The impetus that got the whole thing moving after some initial hesitation was, as so often, emotional. We received a number of telephone calls from commercial architects asking for advice and addresses so that they could contact the appropriate offices in the Berlin administration and start building. They always had an investor ready and most of them had a project as well. Apparently they only needed the site. The city looked like being sold out. And it was not just any city, it was one so rich in tradition, in history; it was the unique, wonderful city of Berlin.

Suddenly everything started moving fast. With Michael Mönninger and our closest staff members in the Museum, we drew up a list of writers and subjects for a series of articles outlining the questions and issues. Entitled 'The New Berlin', these appeared from November 1990 in the *Frankfurter Allgemeine Zeitung*. We also drew up a list of architects to be invited, those we believed were the best worldwide and who seemed to us predestined for the theme. We wrote to them, explained the task and sent them the appropriate planning material. The answers came back immediately and with very few exceptions they were enthusiastic. We could offer nothing but a little support and some publicity. We also offered these to architects who no longer need either. But it was a matter of Berlin, and the truly epoch-making task of redesigning the heart of one of the greatest cities in Europe. The challenge proved fascinating, and the project had started.

That we can now present the results in an exhibition, this magazine and a catalogue is thanks to the co-operation of many people. Michael Mönninger started the project, with myself. In the German Architecture Museum, Volker Fischer and Anna Meseure helped to design and produce the exhibition and the catalogue. Gerd Hatje, for many years my publisher and friend, published the catalogue in a shorter time than anyone ought to be asked to publish one. The authors and architects worked with understanding and involvement and above all with concrete input.

A word on the architects and their work, and so the core of the entire undertaking: it would be unjust to them to underestimate their work and see it as light, rapid sketches. All the ideas are carefully considered and worked out with great exactitude. It would also be unjust to overestimate the work and see these as architectural or planning projects. Not only was the time too short for that (we wanted to get ahead of the speculators and commercial architects), but the programme was also too vague (in most cases it was not even clear to whom the sites in question belonged and what they were to be used for). The architects have produced concrete ideas in concrete form. They should be seen and assessed as such. Naturally they can also be criticised. Criticism is necessary, it helps to identify what is possible, develop and assess alternatives and improves the final results. So we are grateful for criticism. Only we cannot accept the criticism of those who always know better, who act from blind prejudice and operate with demagogic abstractions where the concrete, real city has to be changed.

The concern is not initially to measure the proposals by what is and what is not possible in Berlin today, nor is it to draw up a quality list and choose the best. We can only see these 17 works as a contribution to the urban development of Berlin; they may be heterogeneous, occasionally even contradictory, but they are absolutely coherent.

It is not too early to deduce from this convolution certain

John Hejduk, 'The Potsdam Printer's House/ Studio'

9

Albert Speer, model of the north-south axis, 1939

Aerial view of the Kreuzberg district, 1945

models for the solution of basic problems in Berlin: how to handle the almost surreal strip that has been freed by pulling down the Wall and clearing away the tank blocks and mine-fields; healing the wounds torn in the historical centre by the mistaken need for representation of the old regime; linking the two urban centres, Unter den Linden and Kurfürstendamm, that have developed in the divided city in the last half century. Models, not more. Making these models into projects will be the most important task for the Berlin government in the next few years and decades.

The Berlin administration does not need advice for this. They have sufficient competence in their own ranks and their own city. If we may nevertheless take the liberty of putting forward suggestions arising from our work on this project, we have four to make. Firstly, the plans for the centre of Berlin which has so unexpectedly become available should acknowledge the historical architectural tradition that has produced so many compact, dense and beautiful cities, full of life, in Europe through hundreds, indeed thousands of years. Secondly, they should fill the waste lands that gape in the urban structure with noble monuments, suitable houses and well bordered public spaces. Thirdly, they should stitch up the wounds that the bombs and the Wall with its death strip have torn in the urban tissue, with determination and without succumbing to the temptation to try to blot out history. Fourthly, they should try to answer the many different questions which the architecture of Berlin raises, with care and a wealth of invention, and without dogmatic ideology. Many plans will remain on paper and will only contribute to that invisible city for which, after all, no lesser figures than Karl Friedrich Schinkel, Peter Joseph Lenné, Martin Mächler, Ludwig Hilberseimer and Hans Scharoun have worked. Some will be realised and, it may be hoped, allow the new and no less great Berlin to rise on the foundations of the old.

THE COMPETITION FOR IDEAS

Berlin, that mythical metropolis of the 20s, immortalised in the literature of Walter Benjamin and Franz Hessel, suffered appalling devastation, first by the allied bombs of World War II and again, shortly afterwards, at the hands of demolition-hungry town planners. The city on the River Spree has never recovered from that devastation: the wall that went up in 1961, severing the city into two distinct parts, also tore deep into its very heart. It cut off major thoroughfares, ripped gaping wounds in the urban structure and relegated once-central areas to marginal positions. Even the *Internationale Bauausstellung* which set out in the 80s to repair the ravaged city could do little to change the way things were. Its influence, after all, was limited to just one part of the divided city and any overall urban planning was a political impossibility.

Since the wall came tumbling down on 9 November 1989, all that has changed. Berlin has become one city again, its life force having proved stronger than the political situation that held sway there for 44 years. Now it is time for the political changes that have already taken place to find their counterparts in town planning and architecture.

The challenge is enormous, the task epoch-making. It involves no less than restructuring the centre of a capital city and major international metropolis which, for utterly incongruous reasons that already, in retrospect, seem almost beyond belief, contains vast empty spaces. The huge lane cut by the wall with its infamous 'death strip' is an oppressive no man's land that winds its way across the heart of the city in an absurd, jagged pattern. Many adjacent plots have remained undeveloped, on others stand new buildings, ruins and sheds one might otherwise expect to find only on the outskirts. All this must – and will – change. The once bustling centre of a passionately loved and passionately hated city which, through a quirk of history, was cast into a kind of suburban limbo for almost half a century is now preparing to return to what it once was. For that it needs an appropriate architectural framework.

This framework is by no means something that the centre of Berlin will automatically attain. Admittedly, with very few exceptions, cities are not designed by architects, but develop by themselves; the driving force is property speculation – something there is sure to be no dearth of in a city already in need of at least 200,000 homes and almost eight million square yards of office space. However, if these energies are to be channelled in a direction that makes urbanistic sense and if they are to be used to the advantage of the city, there has to be a plan. In other words, an overall concept is required as an umbrella under which the various projects to create the new city can be brought together.

In order to achieve such a concept, the Deutsches Architektur-Museum, in collaboration with the *Frankfurter Allgemeine Zeitung*, invited 25 prominent architects from all over the world to place their experience, knowledge and creativity at the service of the city of Berlin. They were asked, on the one hand, to propose a new overall urban development concept for the central area between Brandenburger Tor and Alexanderplatz and between Lustgarten and Mehringplatz and, on the other hand, to give examples of architectural solutions for specific individual problems within this particular area. The aim was to produce draft concepts which would not only treat urban development and architecture as an inseparable unit, but also act as a potent source of impetus for restructuring the historic centre of one of the world's great cities. As some fundamental questions regarding Berlin's future – especially in respect of the use and ownership of much of the real estate – remain unresolved, there could, as yet, be no question of drawing up detailed solutions for specific places. Instead, the intention was to draw up general concepts for restructuring the historic centre which should be indicative of an overall solution for the entire area quite apart from any specific problems. The time available was intimidatingly short. We had no intention of staging a purely academic exercise that would merely add still more useless papers to the mountains of unbuilt architectural designs that benefit only specialist periodicals and art galleries. Our aim was to intervene in the actual plans for the city which, in all probability, is to be the capital of a unified Germany. That meant being quick off the mark. We knew that the property speculators and commercial architects were already knocking at the doors of Berlin's politicians with the first – and far from the last – of their opportunistic projects.

Selecting the architects was no easy task. We wanted to invite only those who had already been involved with Berlin or at least with the kind of historic European city of which Berlin is one of the most impressive examples. We wanted to invite renowned and established masters as well as some young architects of whom we had reason to expect greater things. We wanted to include all the major architectural trends which add so much variety and vitality to today's cultural panorama – irrespective of our personal preference. Moreover, of all those trends, we wanted the most radical, the most original – in short, the best representatives. We addressed our invitations according to these criteria: Mario Bellini, Coop Himmelblau, Peter Eisenman, Norman Foster, Frank Gehry, Giorgio Grassi, Vittorio Gregotti, Zaha Hadid, Jacques Herzog and Peter de Meuron, John Hejduk, Steven Holl, Josef Paul Kleihues, Hans Kollhoff, Rem Koolhaas, Daniel Libeskind, Rafael Moneo, Eduardo Souto de Moura, Jean Nouvel, Alvaro Siza, Manuel de Solà-Morales, Aldo Rossi, Oswald Matthias Ungers, Bernard Tschumi and Robert Venturi.

No list of invitations – least of all this one – can claim to be objective. Many outstanding architects whose only handicap was the fact that they had not yet worked in or in relation to Berlin had to be dropped; in the short time available (and with the extremely meagre resources at our disposal) it was not possible to brief them on the task in hand. Many good friends and excellent designers fell by the wayside, often for no other reason than the fact that their stance was already represented by someone else – not necessarily by someone better. We deliberately sought to present examples rather than taking an encyclopedic approach. We did not want a supposedly comprehensive cross section of the international architectural scene, but a small, easily identifiable and quite remarkable group. We

did not want to drum up an army, merely gather a commando to tackle what was virtually a mission impossible.

Fortunately, very few were daunted. Virtually all those invited accepted the challenge: with no money, with far too little time, on the basis of material which we had gathered painstakingly, but in a great hurry. We are not the ones to judge whether this adventure was worthwhile: we are, after all, biased.

Much depends not only on the designs submitted, which we are now presenting, but also on what will be made of them. We hope, for ourselves, for the designers and for the city of Berlin, that they will provide considerable food for careful thought. We hope they will be understood and judged for what they were intended to be right from the start: as fragmentary programmatic manifestos, as collected ideas and concepts, as initial attempts at solutions; *not* as fully fledged solutions. We hope that in selecting ideas which have to be further elaborated with a view to realisation, the result will not be a pot-pourri of solutions, but a clear decision in favour of a single solution: in other words, that a coherent architectural and urbanistic approach can be achieved (which of course, may well reflect the views of more than one person). We hope that once a coherent and clearly defined plan with a carefully balanced variety of architectural styles has been achieved, that which is surely the foremost aspect of Berlin's intellectual heritage will prevail: its tradition as a city of tolerance.

Whatever may follow on from this project, we feel it has certainly been well worthwhile giving some thought to Berlin. We hope that the city of Berlin will accept this gift from 20 of the world's best architects in which we play only the role of enthusiastic mediator. It is an unusual gift, fragmented, unwieldy, perhaps even disquieting. It is nevertheless dedicated to a city which has a responsibility, not only towards itself and Germany, but also towards the whole of Europe – perhaps even the world.

Plan of the areas of the IBA, 1984: Tegel, Prager Platz, Southern Tiergarten, Southern Friedrichstadt and Kreuzberg

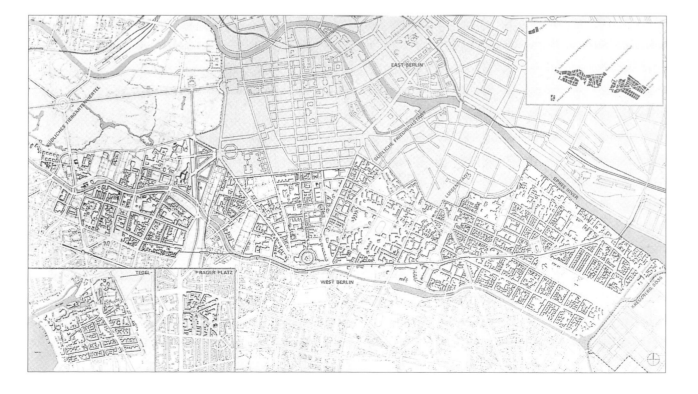

11

VOLKER FISCHER & ANNA MESEURE
IDEAS FOR THE HEART OF A GREAT CITY

Jean Nouvel, 'The Meeting Line'

The Architectural History of Berlin – A Foil for a Competition of Ideas

Berlin has a history of more than 700 years. First the city consisted of two places – a fishing village and a trading centre. Soon it became the residence of a Renaissance prince, and he made it a military camp and then a fortification. After that, Berlin was the capital of a kingdom and when the Second German Reich was established it became the capital of the Kaiserreich. All these historical phases have left traces in the city ground plan.

From the turn of the century the growth of the city, which had been largely uncontrolled till then, was increasingly subject to planning regulations. Undesirable developments, like the typical Berlin tenements with their negative social consequences, caused architects and planners to evolve new models for the future growth of what was then the biggest industrial city of the 20th century – the competition held in 1910 for Greater Berlin was already conceived for a city of at least five million inhabitants. One of its main points was the redesign of the railway network, with eight large terminal stations, some of which are still significant features of the urban scene today. This competition created the basis for the administrative merger in 1920 of the various districts to make the single community of Greater Berlin.

More influential was the 'Section of the Greater Berlin Building Plan' presented by Martin Mächler in 1917. Mächler proposed that all the ministries and foreign representations, that had until then been spread around the city, should be grouped around the Platz der Republik (formerly Königsplatz) or least in its vicinity. His plan also laid particular stress on the redesign of the railway stations, and it already contained a proposal for an underground rail network with a cross-shaped central station. Most important, it envisaged a broad north-south axis, which should play an eminently symbolic role, as well as linking the southern and northern parts of the city – the existing 'absolutist' east-west axis was to be demonstratively crossed.

This idea for a north-south axis, which was to link the districts of Moabit and Wedding with Schöneberg and so fill a serious gap in the urban network, persisted. For there was also a political need for large-scale urban planning. The government had been moved to Weimar in 1918, but this was never intended to be permanent. Berlin remained the centre of political power and the control centre for economic decision-making.

In the 20s mainly large new residential districts were built, combining elements of the English Garden City movement with the language of New Building. Examples are the Britz estate of 1,000 housing units, and 'Uncle Tom's Cabin' with 15,000, by Bruno Taut. The cosmopolitan sophistication and vitality of Berlin in the 20s was crushed by the Nazis, who indulged in huge megalomanic projects in a sterile Neo-Classical style on the one hand and cultivated the petty bourgeois 'Heimat' style on the other.

After the war the gaping wounds in the western part of the city were filled up, as in other West German cities, with functionalist container architecture, more space for which was created by unparalleled demolition. Siemensstadt and Gropius-Stadt are examples of this. In the eastern part, whole historical quarters had to give way to large-scale frame and panel constructions oriented to Stalinist concepts in urban planning. In the name of 'socialist progress' masses of faceless standardised buildings were put up, blurring all contact with the density and functional complexity of the historical city. Now that the wall has come down, the tissue of the city needs to heal again, on the basis of the complex historical development with its living axes, sequences of squares and 'significant places'. Berlin today has a unique historical chance to correct the depersonalisation and loss of identity in both the inner-city satellite towns in the west and the sterile large-scale planning in the east. It needs a careful renovation in the full awareness of the historical context. To a limited extent this was realised in the 80s in the western part of the city by the International Building Exhibition, with its exemplary work. But politically it was not possible to offer planning for the whole of the city, and precisely for that reason this should and must be done in Berlin today.

The Wall as Focus for New Inner-City Planning

In November 1989 what was hardly believed possible happened and the Wall was breached. Week by week new provisional crossing points were opened and the people flooded through, in hundreds of thousands, from east to west and back again. The unstoppable demolition of the wall accelerated – assisted rather sarcastically by the 'wall woodpeckers'. Today only a few dozen metres are still standing of what used to be 46 kilometres of 'anti-Fascist protective fortification' built in 1961. The Brandenburg Gate, at least as important a feature of the city as the Victory Column and the long east-west axis of Heerstrasse – Strasse des 17 Juni – Unter den Linden – Karl-Marx-Allee, is open again and people can walk and drive through it. Checkpoint Charlie, once the symbolic location for the 'spy who came in from the cold', has gone and it may be hoped that Friedrichstrasse will again be the centre of the European theatre, film and cabaret world as it was in the 20s.

Now the arbitrary truncation of streets and axes, squares and green parks, transport and railway links will be as evident as the big empty spaces to the right and left of the old sector border. The political division of the city took no regard for the historical development of the districts and urban structures, it tore deep wounds and pushed a central urban area into a marginal position. Both Pariser Platz at the Brandenburg Gate and the ensemble of Leipziger and Potsdamer Platz were formerly architectural centres of pulsating urban life. They have either been degraded to conveyor belt architecture (around the Brandenburg Gate) or have remained, like the asphalt octagon of Leipziger

Peter Eisenman with Jaquelin Robertson, Social Housing, IBA, corner of Kochstrasse and Friedrichstrasse, 1985-86

Hans Scharoun, Apartments, Wilmersdorf, 1929-30

Platz, on a green no-man's land, only ghostly monuments. Buildings once integrated in a dense urban scene, like the Martin-Gropius-Bau on the Prinz Albrecht site, have throughout the entire post-war period been isolated relics of what was once urban continuity. The waste land, which can stretch for kilometres on both sides of the inner-city border, still goes like a meandering scar through the city, separating in the centre the districts of Tiergarten, Mitte and Friedrichshain. Repairing the urban fabric here between east and west is one of the greatest future challenges for the urban planners in Berlin.

The Inner-City Complex in the Centre of Berlin

Like hardly any other major European city, Berlin developed over a period of 300 years from quite independent districts, each with their own character, to a cohesive whole. The most important extensions to the medieval core of the city start with Baroque Dorotheenstadt (1688) and Baroque Friedrichstadt (1748), and continue with the Neo-Classical arrangements by Karl Friedrich Schinkel and Joseph Lenné (both early 19th century). It is evident even from these extensions, only part of which were realised, that axes and squares were the dominant reference points in the planning considerations. The plans for Dorotheenstadt and those for southern and northern Friedrichstadt all have Unter den Linden as their main axis. One end of this culminates in the 'Quarre', an open space, and the other in the Lustgarten before the royal palace, past Kaiserplatz, the university and the Armoury (Zeughaus). Leipziger Strasse, which runs parallel to Unter den Linden, ends in the Octagon in the east and the Spittelmarkt in the west, while the Rondel lies south of it, with the main roads Potsdamerstrasse, Wilhelmstrasse, Friedrichstrasse, Markgrafenstrasse and Jerusalemerstrasse radiating from it like the fingers of a hand, cutting the cross-axes, some of which extend down to the bend in the Spree. They have helped to create the famous Berlin block system, which began in the centre. The Quarre, the Octagon and the Rondel were planned as a geometrical ensemble – square, octagon and circle – and they were to remain of definitive significance for the shape of the inner city of Berlin right into our century. The Quarre became Pariser Platz with the Brandenburg Gate, the Octagon became Leipziger Platz, with Potsdamer Platz and the Potsdam Gate following on from it, while the Rondel became Belle Alliance Platz (now Mehringplatz). Subtly, the dimensions of the one public place emerged from the preceding, in absolutist urban design, which, although it regulated, also enhanced what already existed. These plans can certainly be compared with other prototypes of centralised royal or aristocratic residences, such as Karlsruhe or Versailles. Schinkel's and Lenné's urban plans accept this basic pattern, even if Lenné stipulated detached houses on the Octagon instead of an unbroken wall of house fronts, and Schinkel on a fitting occasion mocked the 'architectural design with pointed angles'. The places, axes and main thoroughfares, avenues and boulevards were among the most clearly defined elements in the urban scene and its presentation of itself in Berlin as in every other metropolis. It was always the aim to establish public communication in a continuous urban experience, which gives quite a different power and effect to pure transport routes or mere residential and shopping streets. The cohesive places in the urban space were key junctions in the street network, they linked sequences of city streets and gave them a definite rhythm. That is how Alexanderplatz, for instance, a concretisation in stone of the urban experience, could become the synonym of metropolitan density.

Today these streets and places at best give a nostalgic idea of what the former urban quality was. The Brandenburg Gate, once a coherent part of its surroundings, stands isolated, as if forgotten, on a piece of waste land. Leipziger Platz is an archaeological remnant, a memory, no more than an asphalt octagon in the strip of green along the old supervision zone. Alexanderplatz is swept empty and concreted over. It has isolated blobs of socialist optimistic architecture dotted in it, the television tower and the container tower of the Hotel Stadt Berlin, the fountain rotating on itself and the cardboard box of the Alex department store clothed in an aluminium network. All are symbols of that terrible socialist belief in progress that removed most of the historical buildings and city structures that had survived the war in a radical clean sweep. But it is all quiet on the western front as well, where the Strasse des 17 Juni passes through the Tiergarten down to the Brandenburg Gate, serving only a single-minded delight in traffic, more of a city autobahn than an inner-city boulevard. The Kulturforum is an urban desert with isolated fragments scattered in it as if by chance, like those on Alexanderplatz, Mies' Nationalgalerie, Scharoun's Philharmonie, and, standing in isolation, the church of St Matthew.

With our senses newly sharpened we can see now that if Berlin wants to do justice to its future task as a European metropolis, as it did in the 20s and 30s, it must take up the traditions of European cities in its urban planning and architecture as well. In the central part of the city particularly, the inner city network of places and axes and lively boulevards, that was once so rich, must be restored. This is not to re-establish a nostalgic 'status quo ante', it is to renew the pulsating urbanity of the interwar years with contemporary means.

The Model for Urban Quality, Urban Culture

From the various descriptions and opinions on metropolitan centres in the 20th century, it is overwhelmingly evident that the experience of the great city is first and foremost intensified experience of the simultaneity of what is not simultaneous, the simultaneous co-existence of different interests, experiences of life, concepts for life. Looking back, Berlin may only have been a world city and a European metropolis for a short period of its history, where cultural influences, from Chicago and Moscow, New York and Paris crossed and intermingled. But during the 20s this city was an indicator of future social and economic developments, watched, as the writer Karl Scheffler said in 1931, 'with attention by the whole world'. And when Heinrich Berl polemicised in 1932 against the 'American Bolshevik' metropolis of Berlin, the protagonists of this republican metropolitan culture, the writers and editors, actors and poets, film-makers, cabaret artists, artists and musicians, not to forget the architects, were carrying the flag of new urban patterns of living and their cultural impact. The rhythm of the big city, the 'pulse of the age', gathered pace, life became ever more intense. An acceleration of all movement was apparent, the traffic moved faster, as the railway was joined by the electric tram and the automobile. And this acceleration of the rhythm of life penetrated the houses, the official bodies, shops, offices, cinemas and theatres. The turnover of goods was faster, the day lengthened more and more into the night, advertising boards lit up the boulevards, variety halls and cabarets, cafes and fairgrounds were the places of recreation, leisure and relaxation – all a 'secondary' nature intended to compensate for the loss of primary nature. A neon culture, whose endless fascination produced nostalgic echoes in films like *Cabaret* by Bob Fosse and Ingmar Bergman's *Schlangenei*. The accelerated rhythm of the big city was also apparent in art. Socially critical, lurid and involved, the artists illuminated the shady side of life in the big city as well; unlike the approach of a cosy naturalism, the environment was now constructed from fragments of observation and individual scenes in every genre, by George Grosz and Otto Dix, Alfred Döblin and Alfred Kerr, Kurt Weil and Lotte Lenya. The patterns of experience which Potsdamer Platz and Alexanderplatz provided became urban synonyms for the more intense experience of the big city.

We believe that the architectural cultures of the past in Berlin, from the Baroque plans of Joseph Lenné and the Neo-Classical structures of Friedrich Schinkel through the successful examples of historicism and the Garden City movement around Hermann Muthesius and the industrial buildings of Peter Behrens, above all the examples of the 20s avant-garde by Bruno Taut, Mies van der Rohe, the Luckhardt brothers and Hans Poelzig, to name only a few, have been decisive stimuli to the architectural discourse of the modern movement. To continue this, if under different conditions, must be the present concern.

Peter Joseph Lenné, plan of residential Berlin showing layout of public gardens, 1843

Martin Mächler, detail of Greater Berlin building plan, 1920

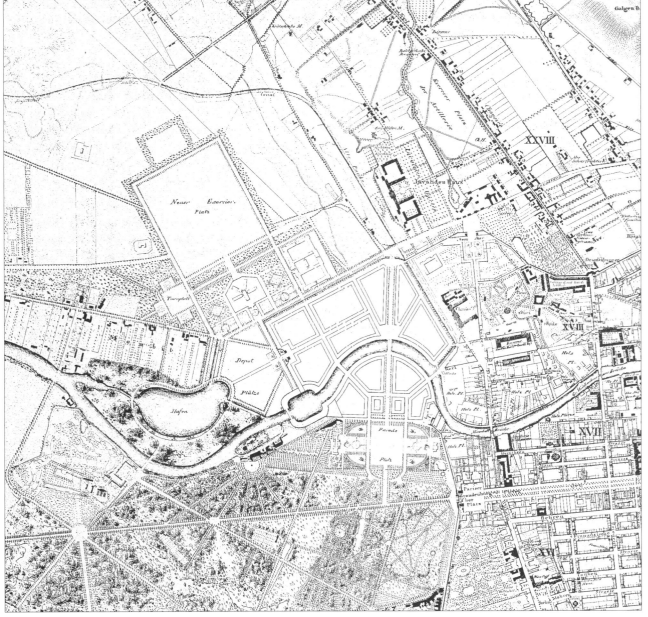

MICHAEL MÖNNINGER
GROWING TOGETHER AGAIN

In 1945 British Air Marshall Arthur Tedder believed that Berlin should be left in ruins, a modern Babylon or Carthage, as a reminder of Prussian militarism and the Nazi regime. The city was dead, he said, one could drive for miles through smoking ruins and see no buildings fit for habitation. Berlin could never be rebuilt, it could only serve as an antique memorial for future generations. 45 years later the monument has become a signpost for the future political and social organisation of Germany, but the third renaissance of Berlin in this century is confronting the city with challenges that no western metropolis has ever known.

Overnight the ground space and population have nearly doubled in the city centre alone. None of the great city planners, from Pope Sixtus V in Rome, through Georges Haussmann in Paris and Daniel Burnham in Chicago to Robert Moses in New York ever had to redesign an urban tissue as damaged as this.

What is developing in Berlin is not picture-book beauty but an exciting city. It can no longer be held together by the uniform ground plans and continuous facades that were characteristic of 19th-century cities, with their muscular technique. Greater Berlin was in any case never planned, but evolved from dozens of villages, many of which do not even have a medieval core. Because 'Berlin reinvents itself every 30 years', as Wolf Jobst Siedler said, it has anticipated the fragmentary character of modern big cities. If the typical German fear of the big city could be overcome, Berlin could embody the new hope for a city that is polycentric, not a monopolistic unit.

For a whole post-war generation, whose awareness and attitudes were formed in regional cities of manageable size, Berlin will provide the first independent experience of a metropolis. As a major middle European centre it will not only become a multi-cultural melting pot, but will also be the incalculable source of conflicts for social opposites. Instead of gradually growing together, the two halves of the city have been abruptly pushed at each other. The explosive impact only makes the previous discrepancy even more painfully apparent. Many underprivileged parts of East Berlin are likely to degenerate into slums, because the rate at which prices are rising is only held back by the wretched state of the buildings and the underdeveloped infrastructure. Not only will more immigrants from Eastern Europe settle in the residential silos of Marzahn, Hellersdorf and Hohenschönhausen, people from West Berlin who cannot cope with the displacement pressure in the more prosperous quarters will move there as well.

The monoculture of prefabricated building has created faceless boxes in East Berlin with tiny windows, in which more than half a million people have to live. The big Marzahn estate, built between 1978 and 1988, has 61,600 apartments; Hellersdorf, built since 1979, has 31,000 so far; Hohenschönhausen (1980 to 1989) a total of 31,000; Altglienicke, the last large-scale building project ordered by the GDR government, was intended to have 17,000. The satellite towns in the West seem almost idyllic in comparison. Gropiusstadt has 16,000 apartments, the Märkisches Viertel 17,000, most embedded in an infrastructure that is intact. In the large East Berlin estates, on the other hand, the only criterion was to build as many housing units as possible in record time in compact structures on open spaces. In most cases the other facilities the people would need were overlooked.

The disdain the Berliners felt for the eastern part of their city even before the war, the cultural contempt for the topography of the more heavily industrialised, proletarian and ethnically disadvantaged districts, are being strengthened by the inferior quality of these buildings and the consequent prosperity gap.

The prognoses of growth in Berlin are staggering. In the next 20 years the city is expected to acquire a further 1.2 to 1.4 million inhabitants, 700,000 jobs and 1.8 million cars. At least 800,000 apartments need to be built. A further 22.5 million square metres of space are needed in addition to this for industrial and commercial use. Because this growth would be beyond the capacities of the city centre, the green belts in the surrounding areas of Brandenburg will probably take the first overspill. The old 'Berlin star', the bands of settlements along the transport routes, radiating out into the environments like a star, will acquire ever new arms and links, particularly southwards, until the carpet of settlements, growing like an octopus, has buried beneath itself an area twice the size of the Ruhr.

The effects of the division of the city that could compensate Berlin for the decades of isolation need to be preserved: the unique outline of its fringe, which embeds Berlin in a largely intact landscape, almost like a medieval citadel. Now that the wall is down the city is expanding in every direction. Only clearly defined regional centres – Potsdam and Brandenburg in the west, Frankfurt an der Oder in the east – could absorb the pressure of expansion. Traditional bureaucratic urban planning alone will not be sufficient to cope with this dynamic, and the growth can only be steered if Berlin develops new strategies for a more effective building and planning policy. Here it could also offer prototypes for other west European cities. There are a number of possibilities: following an old Berlin tradition, the city could re-create the non-political post of Senator for Building who could mediate between investors and the needs of the city. 'Design teams' on the Dutch model could be set up, or the planning could use information techniques and computer simulations to bridge the gap between design and execution and enable a continuous decision-making process.

The rush to obtain premises in the centre, between Alexanderplatz and Kurfürstendamm, making this the future commercial district, may understandably be music to the ears of the city government, which is facing bankruptcy, but if the painful lessons of German post-war urban planning are not avoided in the centre, the periphery will really

Leipziger Platz, 1990

Potsdamer Platz, 1966

be in a sad state. Monofunctional office and business quarters have almost emptied city centres from Atlanta to Frankfurt am Main; they separate life and work, displace inhabitants and make millions into commuters. Munich and Paris, by contrast, have only allowed office centres on their fringes, in the Arabella Park, for instance, and La Défense. This has kept the city centre part-residential, if only with astronomical rents.

Fortunately Berlin has long had similar plans for avoiding distortion. Around the city, along the S-Bahn ring, which is also to be made into a *boulevard périphérique* for road traffic when it is completed in the east, the administration has designated a ring of nine high-quality development focal areas, and for some of these the planning has already started.

These reserve areas in the 'Berlin ring' consist of large old industrial sites, harbour and railway facilities and transport junctions. From the west, moving clockwise, they include: the Westkreuz and the planned over-building of the Halenseegraben, the extension to the Trade Fair site and the construction of a 'teleport' on the ZOB bus station beside the Sender Freies Berlin radio station; the City Westend area between Charlottenburg and Siemensstadt; the West harbour, from which shipping is to be shifted south to the Teltow canal and into a new harbour in the east; the Wedding underground rail station, the Schering site and the Nord railway station; the area around the Leninallee underground station (which is already earmarked for the Olympics): the Ostkreuz at the Ost railway station; the Spree Valley between Berlin-Mitte and Köpenick; Templehof airport; and finally the Schöneberger Kreuz, where the existing autobahn cloverleaf crossing is to be demolished.

Berlin planners have already developed a master plan with the slogan 'Caution in the centre, strong on the fringe'. If it proved possible to focus the pressure of investment for monofunctional shopping and office centres here, these satellite towns could play a much stronger role in forming the city Potsdamer Platz and Leipziger Platz.

A dispute is in progress there on the distribution of the building masses for the first and largest of many future investment projects: the Daimler-Benz service centre, which is to be a quarter of a million square metres. Welcome as the decision was by the head of the concern in Stuttgart to play a pioneer role in building up Berlin, any concentration of pure office space in the city centre is risky. The formal requirements that no building should be higher than the traditional Berlin cornice height of 22 metres and that the historical street line must be respected are simply being blurred over at present, but the architecture will not be able to compensate for the functional risk to the centre.

The Berlin architect Hans Kollhoff has vehemently criticised the compensatory aesthetics of the so-called human scale that will probably be offered here, and the project he presents is designed accordingly. Instead of the typical 'squat and dumpy' Berlin architecture, considerable ground space would be saved if Daimler-Benz were to build a slender tower the size of the Chrysler building in New York. It would offer the same amount of usable space and keep the surrounding area free for more differentiated use. With the old antipathy to tower blocks, which even Mies van der Rohe was made to feel, Berlin will never achieve the metropolitan density of international big cities.

But the privileged centre will have little difficulty in finding investors and appropriate metropolitan architectural concepts. Only in the fringe areas, where no investor

would willingly set costly, high quality buildings, will the ability of a planning policy to cover the whole of the city be tested. The centre can at best serve as a standard of measurement for the entire area. Its architectural and functional qualities will have a magnetic effect on the fringes; they will act as models or provide lively competition, as the various parts of the city defend themselves with all their might against being bled to death. To progressive architects the ideal image of a city has long ceased to be a homogeneous area with a recognisable centre, and it is now seen as competition between fragments. Oswald Mathias Ungers has worked out his concept of an 'urban archipelago' for Berlin, although it is dominated by a very arbitrary architectural language of 'retroactive' historical designs. Ungers pleads for a pluralist, polycentric concept of clearly differentiated islands in the sea of the metropolis, in which each can find the place of his choice. Peter Wilson once said metaphorically, with regard to Tokyo, that the city of the future could be compared to a holographic plate, which has a piece of the whole stored in each fragment.

Berlin already has multiple centres of totally different aspects. No greater contrast is conceivable than that between the incunabula of the 50s, the relaxed Hansa quarter on the Tiergarten and the severity of Stalinallee, now Karl-Marx-Allee. The neo-historical residential building in the east turned away from the new city centre in the 70s and 80s, just as ruthlessly as the post-modernity of the International Building Exhibition, whose suburban scale rejects the future centrality of this part of the city. Only the complete dissolution of the area around the landscape of Alexanderplatz, which recalls Brasilia, and the desert of the Kulturforum have created comparable configurations of an inverted modernity in the two halves of the city.

East Berlin's centre between the Foreign Ministry and the Television Tower is a cemetery of abandoned monuments. Anyone who is not hooked on the illusion of total demolition and rebuilding, which would be economically impossible and culturally impermissible, must accept this funeral pyre; it is an archeological layer, and any future urban structure must be based on it, correcting and supplementing. A new branch of planning that is increasingly claiming attention among architects would prove helpful here, the transformation of the planning sins of the 60s. Such concepts have already been worked out and realised in part for buildings like the unimaginative Equitable tower in Manhattan or the cheerless satellite towns in Amsterdam (Bijlermeer) and Paris (Melun Sénart).

The scope for designing the city is immense, despite the economic downswing, the urgent need for housing and the speculation in building. Half of the land in Berlin is in public ownership, twice as much as in other West German cities. This gives the city government a position and influence that will permit no excuses to be made on the 'inherent dynamic' of the development and the impossibility of steering private investment. Soon the Berlin budget will lose every second D-Mark in its current tax revenues, because the Federal government grants – which totalled DM 13 billion in 1989 – will come to an end. Then the city will need a good management to find more viable financing concepts than the squandering of public assets to which the West German municipalities are so prone before elections in order to conceal their budget deficits.

In future, urban planning in Berlin will necessarily be closely integrated with economic policy. The current orientation to models like Silicon Valley, the London Docklands and other service centres could, however, be fatal for

Berlin. It is still the biggest industrial city in Germany and it has a production potential that now needs support and development. The impressive panorama of industrial buildings near the river, particularly on the Upper Spree, has only become a focus of public attention again since the wall came down. Admittedly, the efforts needed to prevent its impending collapse will have to go far beyond urban planning issues.

For that reason the designs published here should not be seen as intervention but as a necessary supplement to the debate over the future of Berlin. They are intended to recall to a Berlin suffering existential *angst* that beyond the immediate needs it must give its new, gigantically growing community an appropriate concept and design. And because this is only possible in conjunction with the economic driving forces, the city must make all the greater efforts – perhaps with the help of these designs – to make the investors aware of their task in shaping the city and its community. Indeed, it must attract them back to Berlin again with high-quality urban spaces and new buildings.

We gave a few spatial and functional instructions to the architects we invited. This laboratory situation seemed to us the only way out of both the overpowering economic considerations in the development of the city and the lifeless functionalism of the social statisticians, with their previously determined areas of use. That most of the concepts do nevertheless complement and supplement each other has changed the competition of ideas into a concert of ideas. The designs attempt to mediate between two extremes: between the call for the general order of a master plan, as in New York, Paris or Barcelona in the 19th century, and the easy capitulation before the chaos of an emergent world city.

With the regeneration of Berlin, many urban enthusiasts are talking happily about the beauty of the old European centres, particularly Paris, but it is hard to proclaim the decade of democracy and human rights after the changes in eastern Europe and at the same time plead for planning methods that are relics of autocratic constitutions. A rigorous unity between urban planning and architecture is ultimately only possible in dictatorships, where large areas can be ruthlessly arranged to order, regardless of property and personality rights.

Anyone who complains of the virtual babble of tongues in the present discussion on the city should not forget that the apparently ugly environment is the expression of a community that has successfully thrown off the chains of political repression. To help us find the way from this partial desertification of our cities to a new democratic consensus in architecture, no city offers a model for this that is richer in architectural history and more open to the future than Berlin.

So far, Berlin has been rather like the eternal heavenly Jerusalem, to which all prayed but in which no-one believed. Now that the city has come back to life overnight it faces the biggest task of its post-war history; shaping a big city that will be a model for the metropolis of the 21st century, ecologically, economically, socially and culturally.

The Spreeufer, 1990

Alexanderplatz, 1990

View from the portico of the old museum

MARIO BELLINI
REVITALISING A MULTIPLE HEART

The reunification of Berlin is indubitably a source of enormous social, economic and infrastructural problems. But if a city is the mirror of its own history and of the culture and aspirations of those who live there, then this sudden and unexpected reunification has laid bare wounds and urban development problems that are far more serious and regrettable.

Half a century after the war, this destruction has been aggravated by senseless demolition and rebuilding and by violent artificial division. Fundamental problems have remained unsolved or have merely been buffered in an attempt to cope with the endless demands of progress (in both west and east) in unspoken anticipation of an end to this utterly absurd situation, unparalleled in the history of any major city.

The infamous Wall has gone: torn down and sold off to tourists in colourful chunks along with the hot dogs: exorcism combined with subconscious cannibalism and subliminated by fetishistic ceremonies.

And yet, the traces of the barrier have never been so visible; they distort the city like an unsightly scar defacing a body that has, until now, been forced to exist with two hearts, two circulatory systems, two heads and two totally contradictory ways of life. West Berlin, above all, was left to its own devices and had to find a new focal point, new monuments, a new balance and new forms of development because it had been cut off from the former centre. In East Berlin, on the other hand, the Wall unnaturally relegated the centre to the margins, where it lost its significance and its weight and had to suffer the insult of the cruel 'modernisations' that followed the laudable repair and rebuilding of the main monuments destroyed in the war. Under these circumstances and within the scope of the 'Ideas Workshop' the topic proposed can meet with nothing but unreserved approval. The reunification of Berlin brings countless problems in its wake. However, the greatest problem is that of revitalising a multiple heart which has regained its unity and now has to seek its identity because it can no longer be what it was 50 years ago.

Kurfürstendamm, the Gedächtniskirche, the Kulturforum, the Philharmonie, the Neue Nationalgalerie, the Hansa-Viertel, the IBA, Kreuzberg, the TV tower and the Karl-Marx-Allee are all part of the reality that has to be faced in defining a new balance. Simply restoring or continuing the *status quo ante* is not only a physical impossibility, but also culturally inadmissible. Our design is subdivided into phases of scale and concretion.

The areas north of the River Spree and south of the Landwehrkanals have to be activated. The two existing main thoroughfares linked with the urban speedway should not be allowed to continue channelling traffic from the west through and around the Tiergarten to the former city centre in the east. The reconstruction of buildings demolished after the war prevents rapid transit through these areas. They remain accessible via a circular bypass and a system of underground car parks.

The importance of the areas to the south of the Tiergarten as a transit zone between this green area and the heavily developed district is confirmed. These areas should be reserved primarily for cultural institutions which have become hallmarks of the new Berlin.

Pariser Platz, Leipziger Platz and Mehringplatz, on the other hand, are to be rebuilt. The blocks of Friedrichstadt are to be brought together again as planned and re-integrated into the hitherto defaced Leipziger Strasse.

Redevelopment of the Museumsinsel: entirely reserved for cultural and academic institutions, the ancient district of Cölln is to become a kind of floating Acropolis. Between the boulevard of Unter den Linden and the medieval city centre, a large complex is to be created in which art and science seek a dialogue with the public.

The new Museumsinsel, with a new, round Kulturschloss ('Palace of Culture') acts as a backdrop to the historic boulevard, like the former Altes Schloss, now with a new typology. A central square, open and diagonally structured, creates a hinge in front of the Altes Museum.

Revitalising the medieval city centre: This part of the city between the S-Bahn railway and the River Spree must be given back its distinctive character by maintaining the pre-war street plan and allowing it to develop into a multifunctional 'village' with a wide range of services and a vibrant street life from morning to night.

Between the new Kulturschloss and Alexanderplatz, in the reintegrated central row of individual buildings, there is to be a system of elevated pedestrian zones. These are linked by covered passageways to a colonnaded square looking onto the Marienkirche and the Rathaus as well as the TV tower, which is to remain.

With a wealth of open spaces and planes, this piazza is to become a symbol of the entire district. It is situated in front of the elevated railway station and has its bridgehead at Alexanderplatz. The new, more appropriate proportions could make this square the focal point of urban expansion in the north-east. We propose that the site adjacent to the S-Bahn railway line should be used for open and covered markets and that a provocative, compact high-rise complex should be built on Alexanderplatz. Not only would this be the only possible background for the incredible, invincible TV tower, but it could also be a realistic source of income, enabling Berlin's vast centre to re-establish itself and to attain, from Tiergarten to Alexanderplatz, the height, density and quality that are the city's most valuable heritage.

With Claudio Bellini, Antonio Esposito, Carlo Malnati, Donato Severo, Lonrenzo Viti. Collaboration: Maria Grazia Angiolini, Elena Bruschi, Giovanni Cappelletti, Chiara Costa, Enza Gueli, Marco Parravicini, Luisa Ravera, Vittorio Samarati.

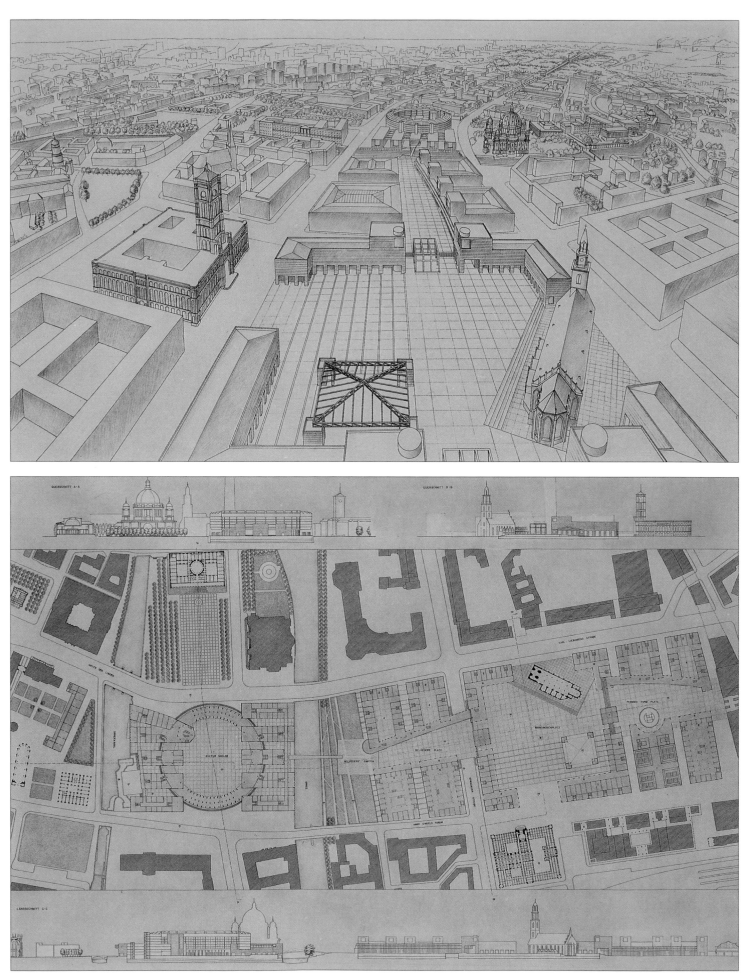

Bird's eye view from the TV tower and site plan

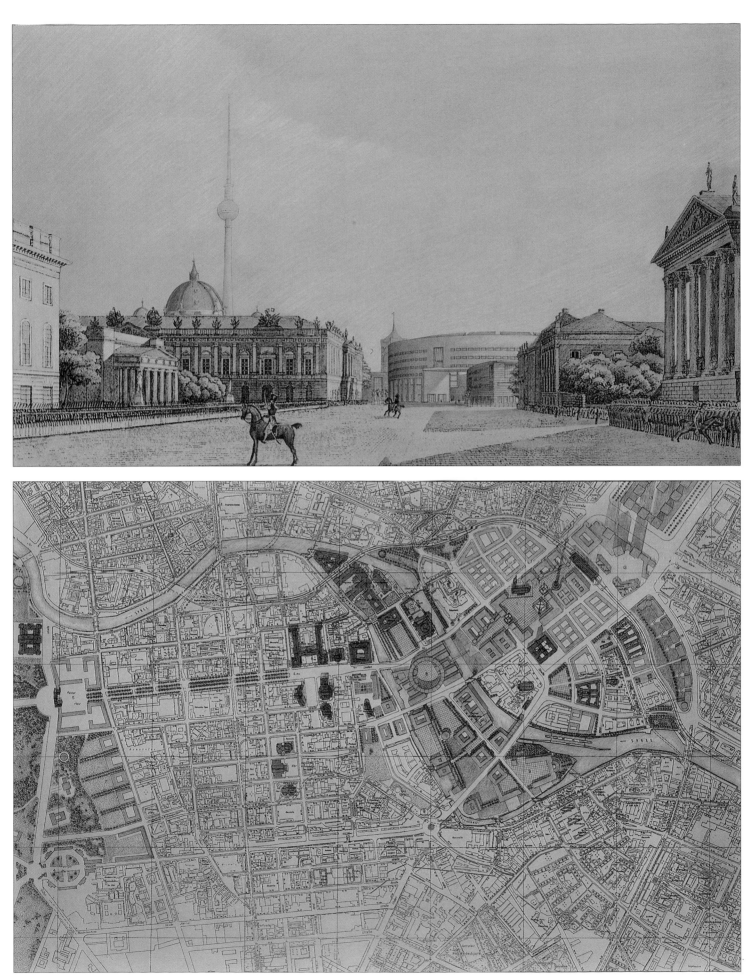

View of Unter den Linden and site plan

23

COOP HIMMELBLAU
CROSSING POINTS

The two halves of the city draw each other together, channelling energies into a line between Theodor-Heuss-Platz and Fischerinsel. The new city will emerge from the combination of an outdated order: East Berlin and West Berlin. The high-speed Paris-Moscow route links Berlin to Europe, creating, together with the inner-city energy line, the basic figure of the concept: Berlin Crossing.

In this figure, which finds its architectural expression in the traffic and transit hubs of the railway station, the dot-like hotel towers are to be built.

Between the railway station and the Fischerinsel (which is to become a leisure district), energy is concentrated on the Leipziger Strasse. Existing buildings are integrated in a multifunctional block according to the 'Para-site City' model with the containers of the 'Developer City' towering in the background. Activated by this combination, infrastructural measures in the form of architectural cores of crystallisation span a field of complex urban forces, setting the process of urban change in motion.

Crossings create points and points create crossings.

Collaboration: Sepp Weichenberger with Klaudia Hornung, Mladen Jadric, Max Kappus, Michael Spieß and Reiner Zettl.

OPPOSITE PAGE: LEFT: Berlin Crossing, Developer City and Developer Parasite Crossing; RIGHT: The Light of Public Space, the Arteries of the City and The Body of the City

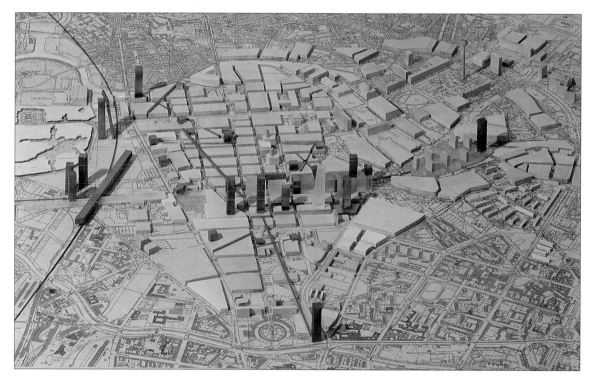

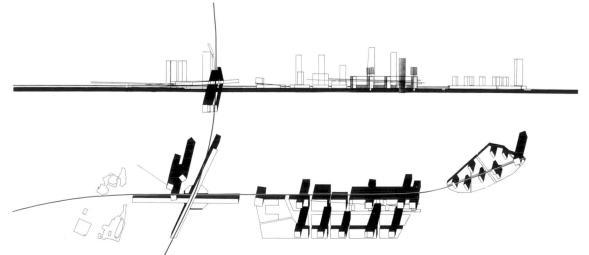

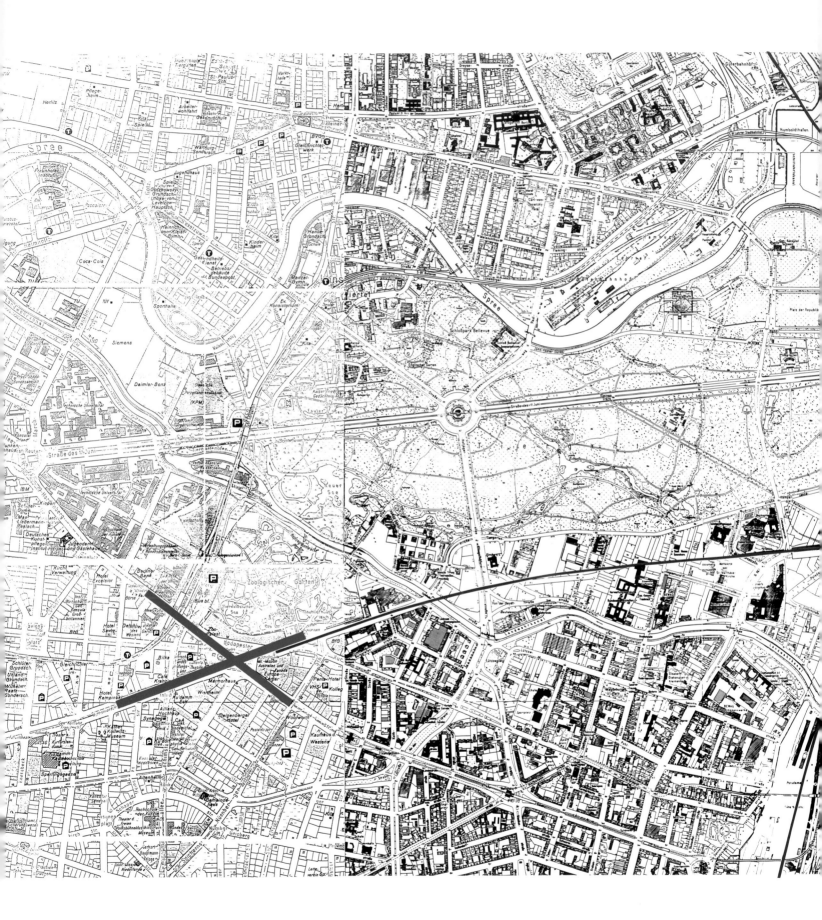

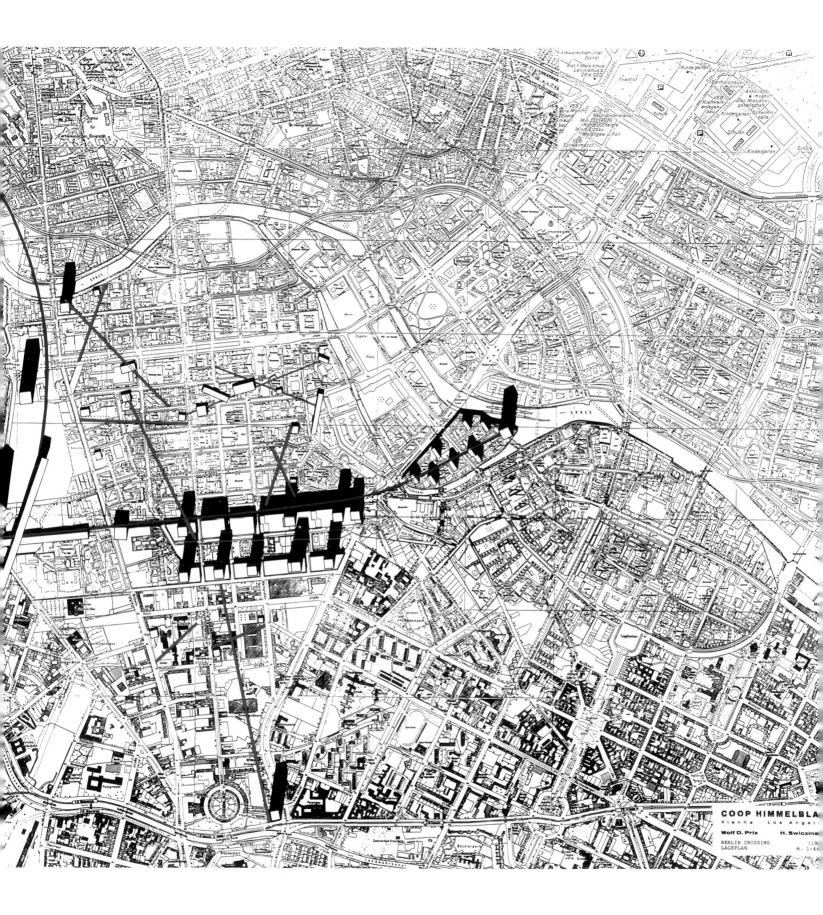

COOP HIMMELBLA
Vienna · Los Angel
Wolf D. Prix   H. Swiczins
BERLIN CROSSING   (19
LAGEPLAN   M. 1:4

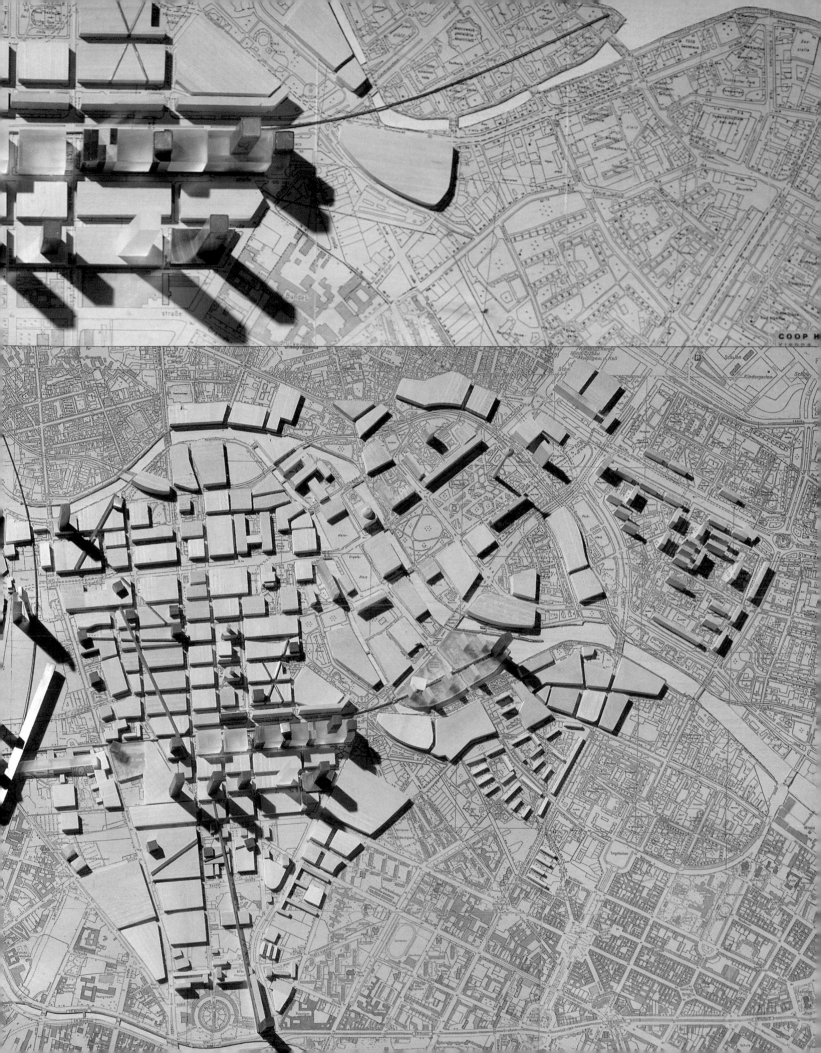

COOP H

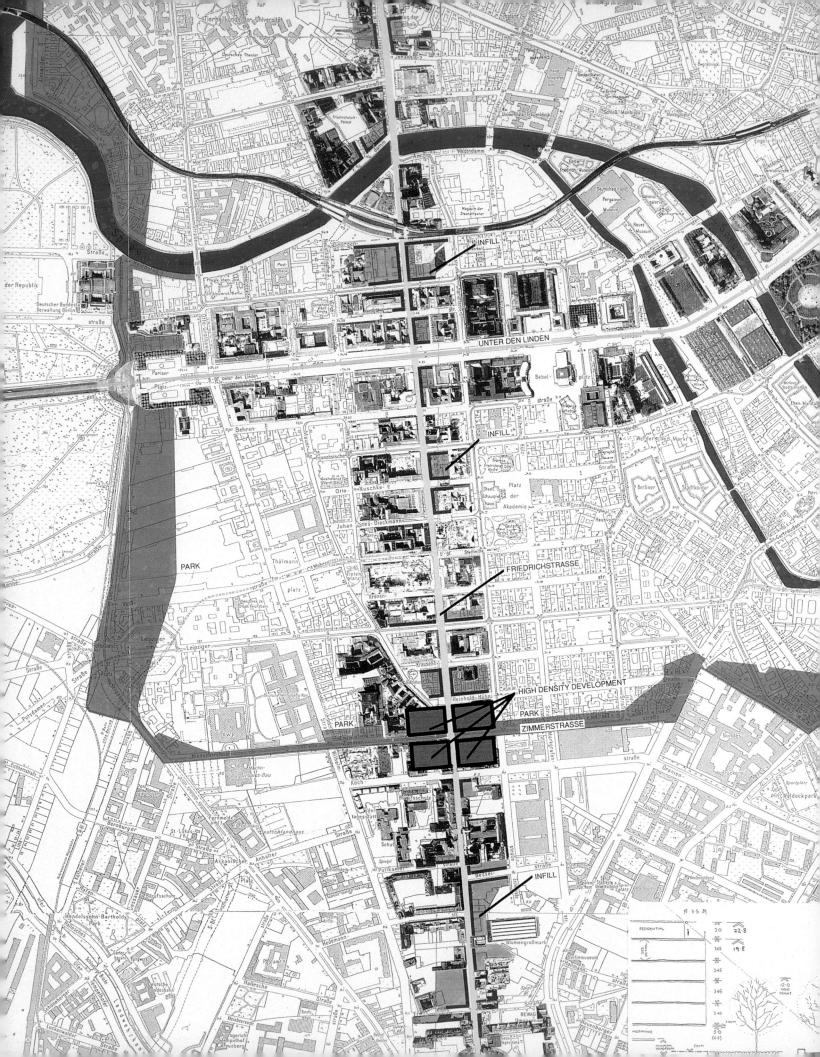

INFILL

UNTER DEN LINDEN

INFILL

FRIEDRICHSTRASSE

HIGH DENSITY DEVELOPMENT

PARK

ZIMMERSTRASSE

PARK

INFILL

RESIDENTIAL

NORMAN FOSTER
BERLIN MASTERPLANNING STRATEGY

The reunification of Berlin has generated a world-wide interest in the city's future development. Municipal authorities have been besieged by planning applications and interested groups, all wishing to participate in the exciting redevelopment. In turn the authorities have responded by implementing a global development strategy. What is urgently needed, however, is a comprehensive strategic masterplan that would negotiate between such an overall approach and the pressures from individual site development. This would allow a very intensive development programme to go ahead in a considered and controlled manner, transforming the city but not destroying its history or its identity.

The location of the Berlin Wall was relatively arbitrary – following the line between one administrative sector and another. However, its world-wide political importance and the events in recent history which have taken place there mean that inevitably it has become part of the totality of Berlin.

To obliterate this area for ever, which is currently the presumed fate of the wall zone, would be to deny to future generations that this part of the history of the city ever existed. It would also mean losing a unique development potential that other cities throughout the world have historically capitalised on. Fortifications around cities in many parts of Europe have been removed when city expansion has overrun them and the need for defence is no longer a priority. This valuable land now at the heart of a larger, higher density community can provide at a relatively low cost new opportunities for public space. By linking this to a controlled development programme which would increase land values around such a public amenity, history can be preserved, new green space in a city created, and high quality development made possible. Frankfurt and Vienna are just two examples of where this has been achieved.

Workshop: After attending the 'Berlin Zentrum' Symposium and having received additional pressure from private developers interested in the renewal of the city, we undertook our own investigation of the implications of unifying East and West Berlin from an urban design standpoint. We revisited the city on a second research trip and evaluated the results in London in the form of an internal design workshop.

History: We started by looking back in time at the historical development of Berlin. The city expanded and changed over the years in a similar pattern to other European centres, but achieved by the early 20th century a very advanced and sophisticated urban integration. Architecture, urban spaces, street patterns, landscape and water interrelated to form a unique town shape and a strong individual identity.

Western Centre: The imagery that Berlin uses to portray itself to others enforces the placement of a western centre to the south west of the Tiergarten. In recent years, this area has developed dramatically in what was an almost isolated city providing a new focus away from the historical centre.

Eastern Centre: Tourist maps of East Berlin illustrate the perceived centre of this part of the city as the remaining historical nucleus. Because of this expansion plans have a predictable and predetermined orientation towards the East.

Historical Transformations: Both eastern and western sectors were damaged by war and political confrontation. However, the basic structure of the city in the form of a strong urban street pattern has remained and must provide the basic framework for future development.

One City: The now reunified city has an eastern and western nucleus: a double focus either side of the Tiergarten. The history and transformations of the past have shaped present circumstances and will influence the future development of the city.

Strategic Plan: In rejoining the two halves of the city it is essential that the street pattern is relinked across the wall zone. Transforming this area of desolated space into a city park generates the potential to stimulate future development around a public amenity.

Sketch Study: A new public open space network for the city, which integrates and enlivens existing city spaces, revitalises river locations and provides a focus for new development, would establish a strong strategic structure for the future progress of the city as a whole.

Friedrichstrasse: The axis of Friedrichstrasse intersects the Unter den Linden and also crosses an area of the wall. *Frankfurter Allgemeine Zeitung* requested that we put forward proposals for this intersection. Having established the strategy of reinforcing the existing street pattern and reconnecting severed east-west road links, the logical development for Friedrichstrasse is to repair the existing fabric of the street. Individual sites would be developed with strong planning guidelines establishing height limits etc, to regain a degree of consistency in the architecture of the street. The only location where this rule could be broken is at the point where Friedrichstrasse crosses the new park. Here, increased plot ratios would stimulate new development fronting this important new urban amenity.

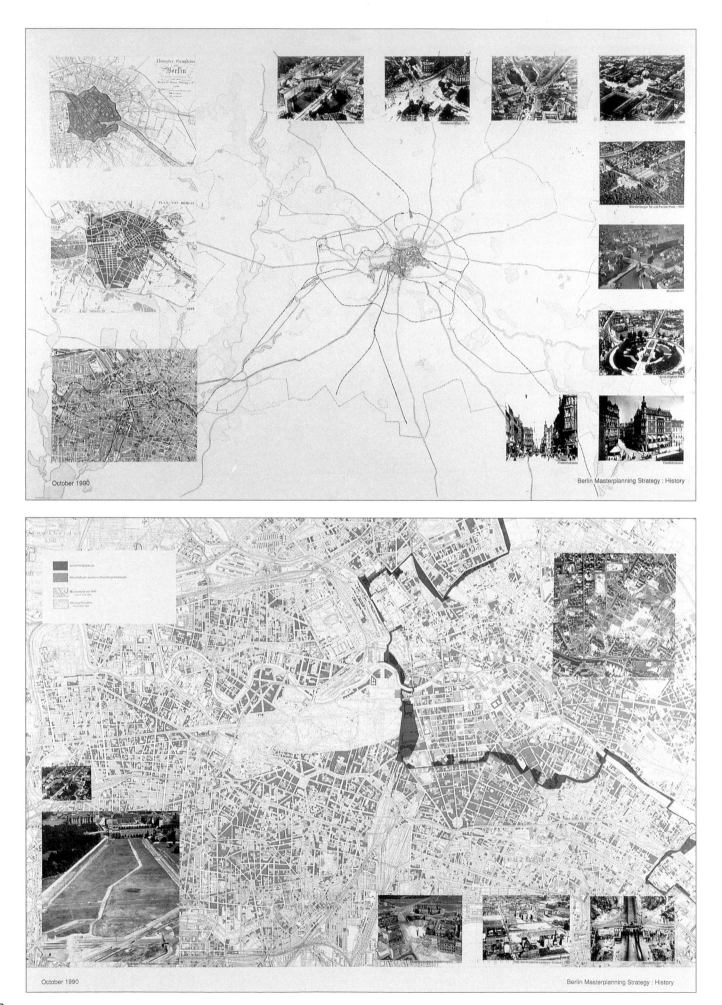

October 1990

Berlin Masterplanning Strategy : History

October 1990

Berlin Masterplanning Strategy : History

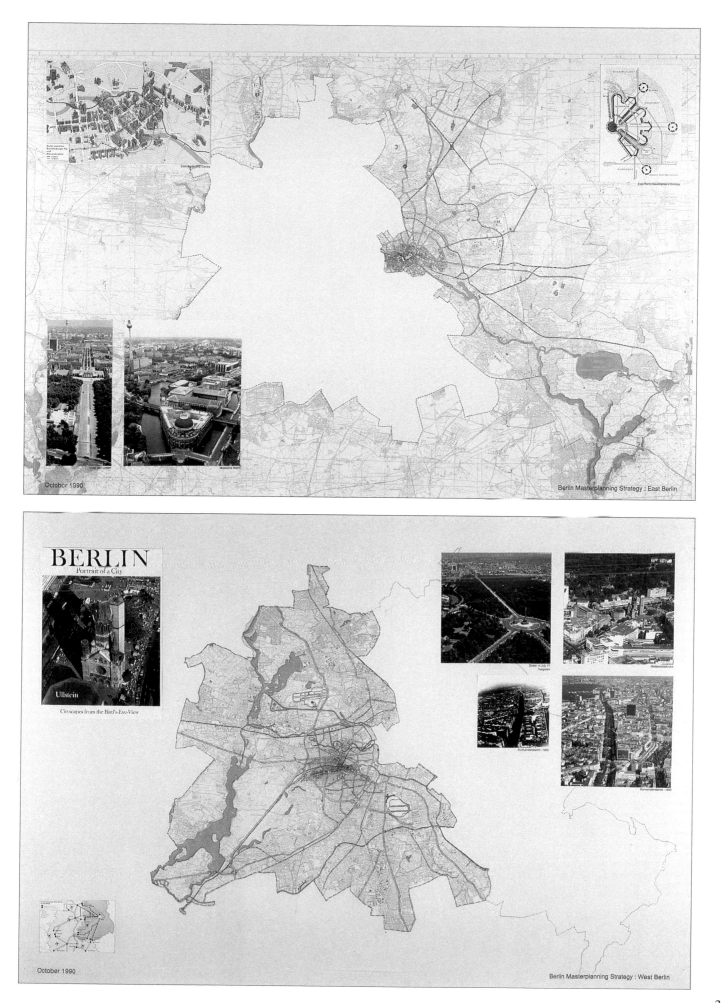

October 1990

Berlin Masterplanning Strategy : East Berlin

BERLIN
Portrait of a City

Ullstein

Cityscapes from the Bird's-Eye-View

October 1990

Berlin Masterplanning Strategy : West Berlin

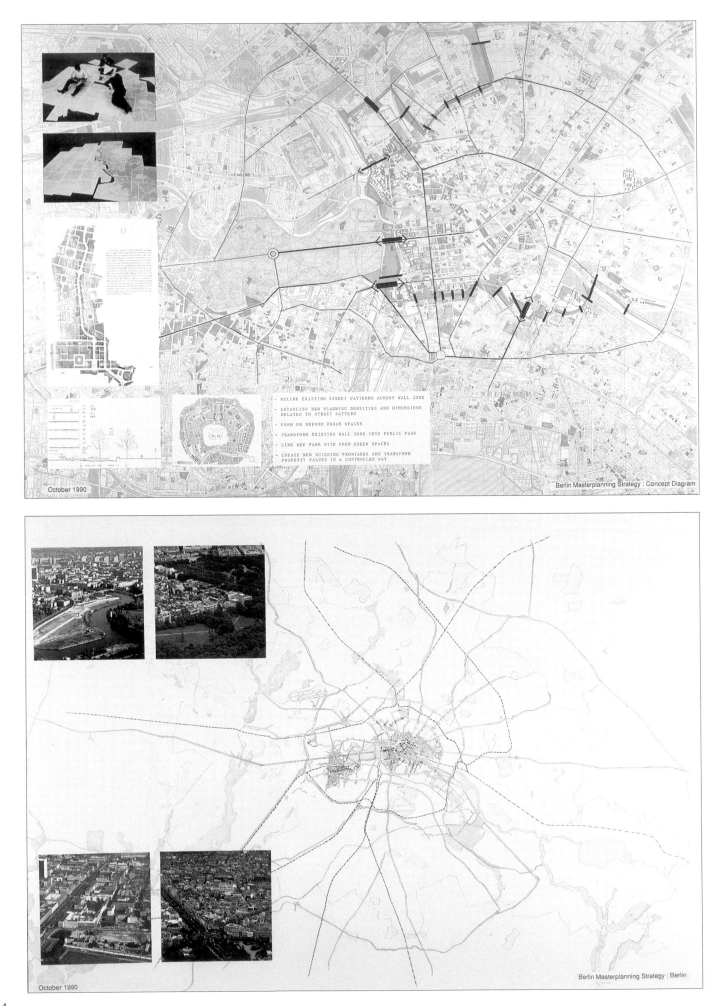

- RELINK EXISTING STREET PATTERNS ACROSS WALL ZONE
- ESTABLISH NEW PLANNING DENSITIES AND DIMENSIONS RELATED TO STREET PATTERN
- FORM OR REFORM URBAN SPACES
- TRANSFORM EXISTING WALL ZONE INTO PUBLIC PARK
- LINK NEW PARK WITH OPEN GREEN SPACES
- CREATE NEW BUILDING FRONTAGES AND TRANSFORM PROPERTY VALUES IN A CONTROLLED WAY

October 1990

Berlin Masterplanning Strategy : Concept Diagram

October 1990

Berlin Masterplanning Strategy : Berlin

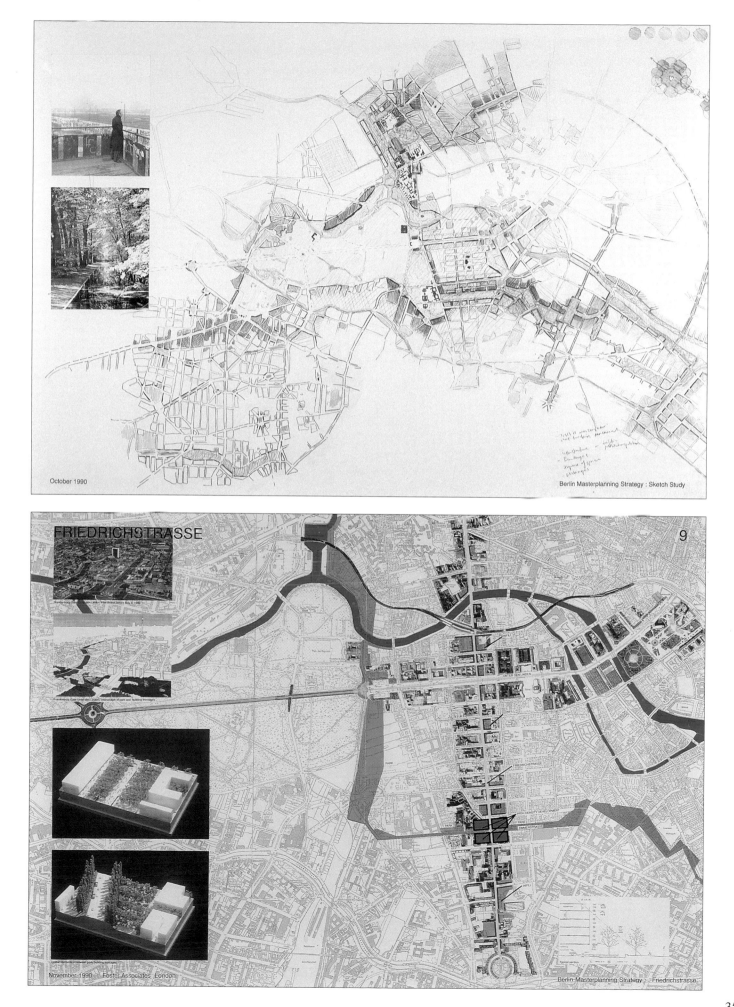

October 1990

Berlin Masterplanning Strategy : Sketch Study

FRIEDRICHSTRASSE

9

November 1990   Foster Associates London

Berlin Masterplanning Strategy : Friedrichstrasse

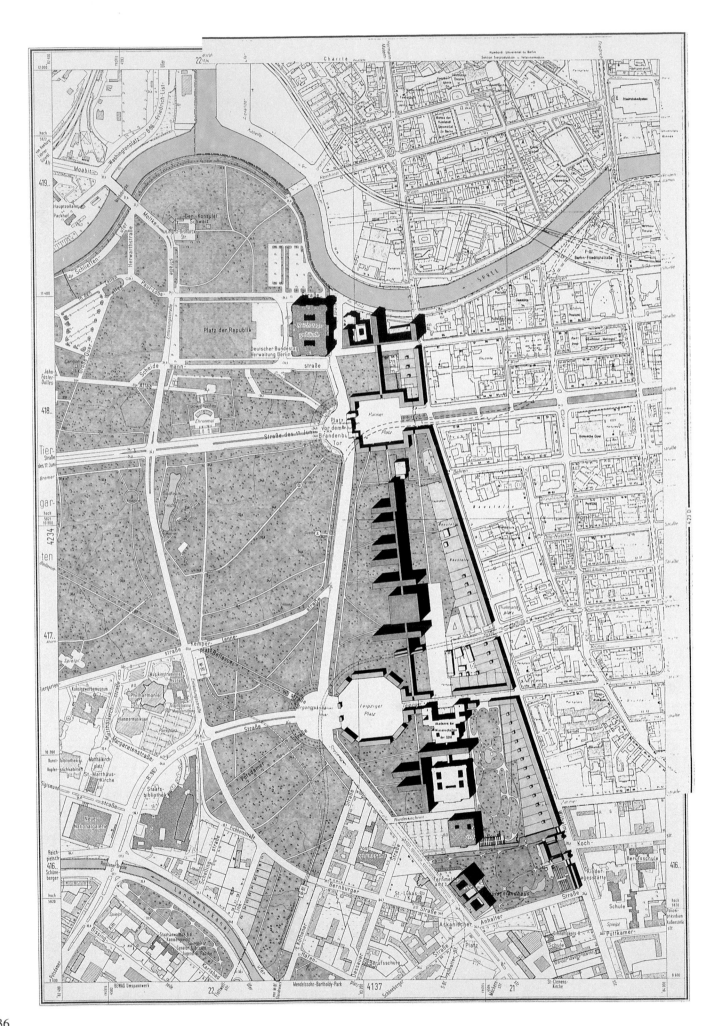

36

GIORGIO GRASSI
SUPERIMPOSING THE OLD AND THE NEW

Our plan involves the urban area bordered in the east by Grotewohlstrasse, in the north by the Reichstag and the River Spree, in the west by the Tiergarten park and Stresemannstrasse, and in the south by the Prinz Albrecht area (the former Nazi government quarter). It centres on a new architectural definition of the western border of the historic Friedrichstadt, possible only now, after the devastation of war and 40 years of division by the Wall. The plan is based primarily on the architectural contrasts of this old district (which has been distorted and remodelled so often that it has lost its original character) and reflects the value and topicality of its original architectural form.

Our project involves superimposing two distinctly recognisable urban types as an expression of the double historic significance of this area: the original ground plan of the former Baroque residential city and the newly designed governmental and administrative buildings of a unified Germany. We propose combining the former residential layout with its typically low-level, unbroken development, with a design for a high, structured city of new governmental and administrative buildings. The result is two distinct and contrasting urban forms which nevertheless harmonise with and complement each other. The city is not to be distorted in order to adapt it to its new function. There is to be no gradual encroachment on the old by the new.

The first concept recapitulates the western borders of the old Friedrichstadt, epitomising the spacious *forma urbis* which characterises Berlin as a city. The second design, both structurally and spatially, complements the first confirming the border between the Tiergarten park and the historic Friedrichstadt. An uninterrupted yet distinct complex of buildings runs north-south, linking the Reichstag with the former Landtag both functionally and visibly, reaching as far as the two Baroque gardens of the former war ministry and the ruins of the Prinz Albrecht Palais, which is to be rebuilt as a museum and memorial (cf IBA competition entry).

The use of two types of plan corresponds to the juxtaposition of two types of building: the street-block construction (three-storey with garden to the rear) which runs along the entire western side of the Grotewohl-strasse and also surrounds Pariser Platz and Leipziger Platz, and the single-level but differently structured complex of major building fragments running north-south on the former garden sites where a large proportion of the new public, political-administrative and representative institutions are to be built.

Two alternative forms develop independently in accordance with their design and redefine the front of the former monumental centre at the edge of the Tiergarten.

Collaboration: Nuncio Dego, Elena Grassi, Enrico Pelloni.

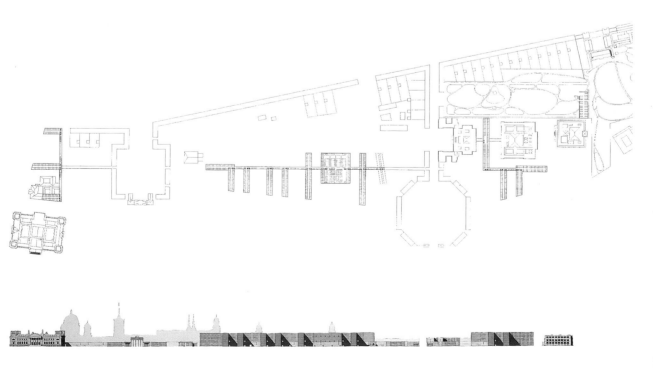

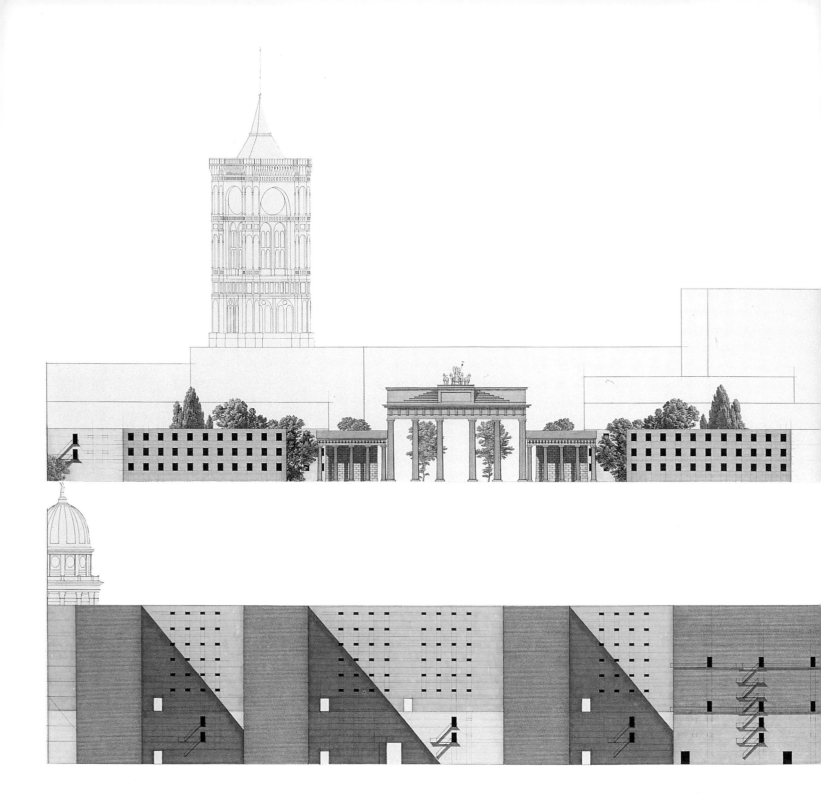

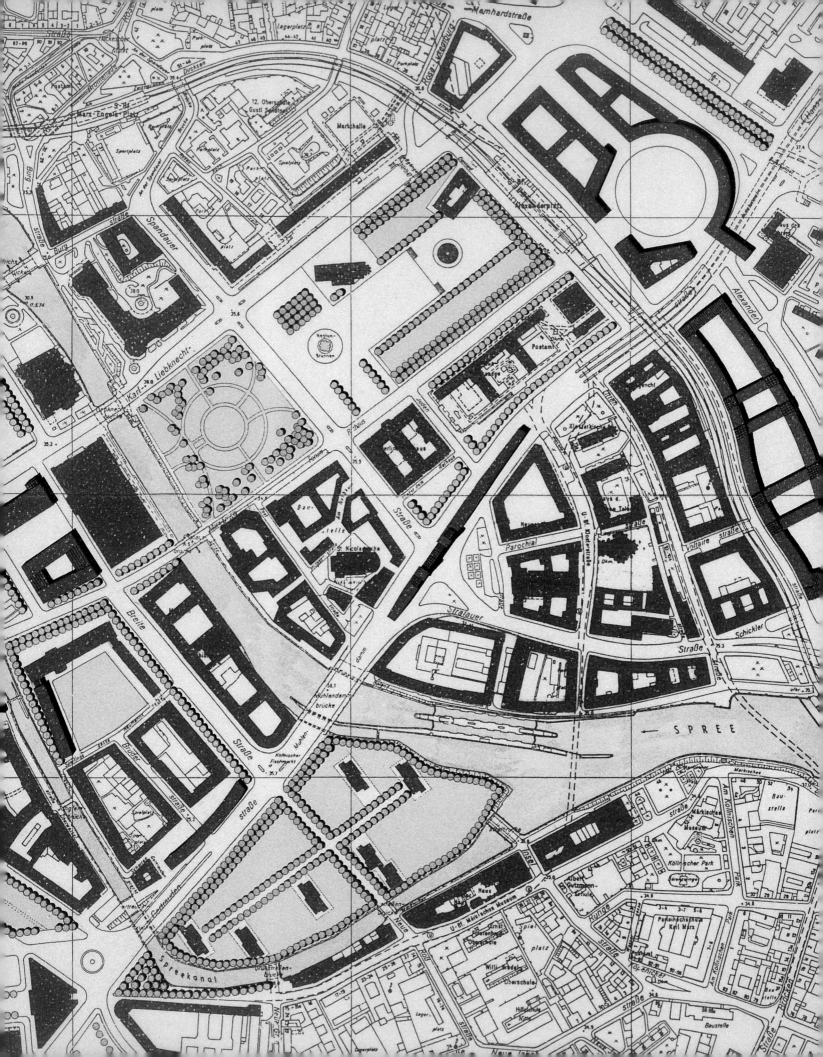

VITTORIO GREGOTTI
GREATER BERLIN

Berlin will become Germany's new capital and will play a key role in the changes taking place in the east. Accordingly, services and infrastructures will be expanded. Closed-down industrial areas will play an important role and will promote the creation of a system of infrastructural hubs along the S-Bahn light railway circuit. The modernised S-Bahn light railway system will gain an increasingly important place in the public transport network, becoming the main link between the city and its suburban communities so that Berlin can become a city of six million inhabitants. The number of public parks should be increased by creating a Tempelhof Park and a new North-South Park. In addition to Tegel and Schönefeld airports, which are to be reserved for special purposes, a new airport is to be built in the west.

The Polycentric City: Although Berlin is a city of the late 19th century, having developed in little more than 70 years as the result of extensive planning, the changes, as in any European city, will be diverse. No single idea will provide the solution, no single vision will hold sway. We present a number of independent proposals for themes and measures which we regard as strategic or exemplary. In the public interest, much will depend on how the unique opportunity presented by publicly-owned real estate in the east is used. The preservation of both city centres will be favoured, their contrasting and complementary characters linked by the new inner-city S-Bahn rail circuit in the new polycentric system. The renewed east-west links have to be extremely efficient without forfeiting the character of the urban avenues.

The North-South Axis: We have taken up the idea of a north-south axis already proposed at the turn of the century and propose a park as a link between the two central areas; the new monuments of the capital city of Berlin are to be erected here. The underground tunnel for the fast Paris-Moscow rail link will run on this axis, as will the north-south motorway connection of the A10. On the site of the former Anhalter Bahnhof railway station, where they briefly surface, there will be a central interchange.

Spittelmarkt: In restoring the street network of Friedrichstadt, for example in the case of the Unter den Linden boulevard, such exceptions as Leipziger Strasse must be accepted. For example, as a large, longitudinal space with the new triangular building at Spittelmarkt in the east and a building in the west on the street axis to close off the existing void.

Only future requirements will determine the kind of changes, demolitions and new developments that existing buildings in the immediate vicinity will undergo.

Stadtmitte: For the central island of Stadtmitte, we propose re-establishing the open spaces opposite the Altes Museum and, to the south, creating a large garden with underground parking, technical and municipal facilities and a shopping centre. To the east of the island, we propose maintaining the large open space opposite the Roter Rathaus and restructuring the base of the TV tower, which is to be retained. Moreover, the Ministry of Foreign Affairs is to be demolished and the Bauakademie restored. Behrens' competition project of 1929 for the Alexanderplatz should be built and an unbroken block created in the area between Alexanderstrasse and the S-Bahn railway line.

The Wall: The area of the Wall should not be eradicated. It is important to maintain the traces and even, in some cases, to modify them as a point of reference for the adjacent areas. In other cases, the void should contribute towards defining the borders of built-up areas or improving communications. However, building should be avoided on the former site of the Wall. At the same time, there should be a drive to increase housing density in the city centre by adding to existing blocks. New buildings, demolitions and conversions will be needed to achieve the envisaged changes of usage meeting current standards of security and environmental protection as well as complying with building regulations.

Collaboration: Paolo Bonazzi, Augusto Cagnardi, Pierluigi Cerri, Pino Donato, Simona Franzino, Elena Galvagnini, Andrea Lancellotti, Fabio Montrasi, Sergio Pascalo, Michele Reginaldi. Consultant: Walter A Noebel.

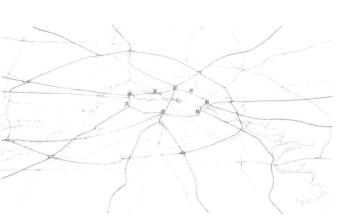

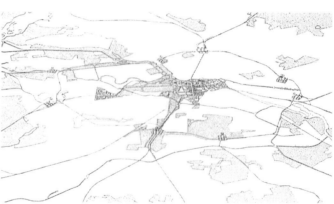

TOP TO BOTTOM: Greater Berlin, The Polycentric City and the North-South Axis

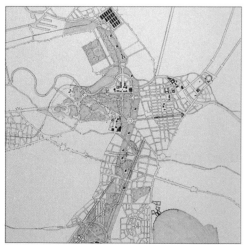

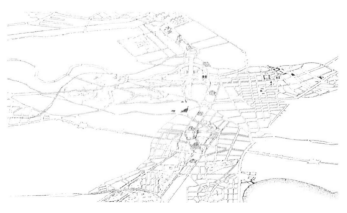

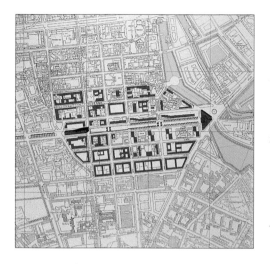

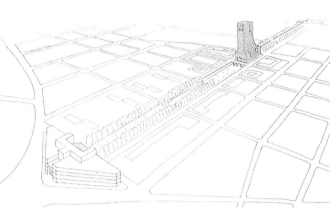

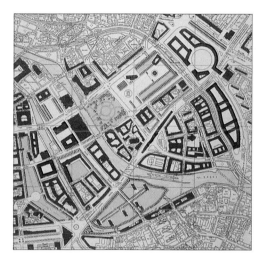

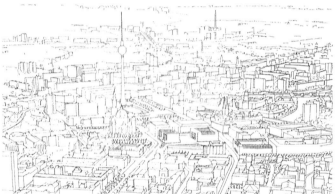

*TOP TO BOTTOM: Spittelmarkt, Stadtmitte and
The Wall*

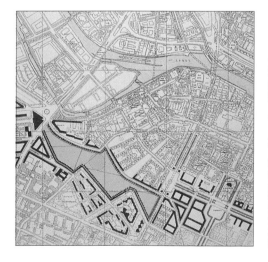

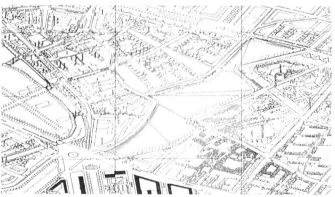

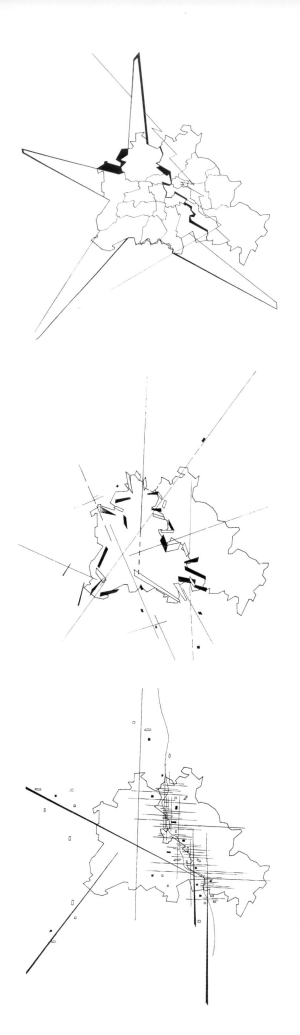

ZAHA HADID
THE DEAD ZONE

The brief for this workshop requested a general strategy towards the existing axes of Mehringplatz to Bahnhof Friedrichstrasse and Brandenburger Tor to Alexanderplatz, and a specific strategy towards a given site.

Our given site was Alexanderplatz for which we adopted a policy of non-intervention because it is one of the few attempts to go beyond the typical 19th-century urbanism. Another site holds importance for us. This is the border line, or dead zone immediately adjacent to the wall. This site must be preserved to prevent it from being covered by homogenous commercial development. The dead zone should remain retrievable as a field across the city, which would allow reinterpretation with a new public programme.

The border line does not have the rectilinear definition of the Berlin block structure. It is delicate, vulnerable and witness to Berlin's separation. To establish the 19th-century Berlin block over this ribbon of non-territory would erase all memory.

The painting lays Berlin open for scrutiny. To the right-hand edge of the painting are placed a series of diagrams, showing possible development of these newly released territories (the wall zone bisecting the City and the former perimeter fence).

The star-shaped plan illustrates the expansion of Berlin to contain its imminent population explosion. New corridor cities project into the landscape. In the lower diagrams, new geometries inhabit the dead-zone, sometimes rectilinear yet slightly out of synch with the existing order. In others they are random and over scaled.

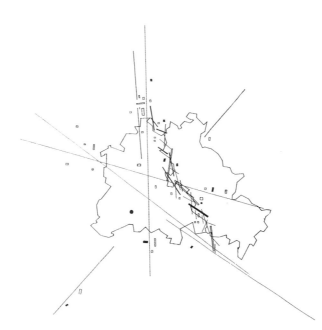

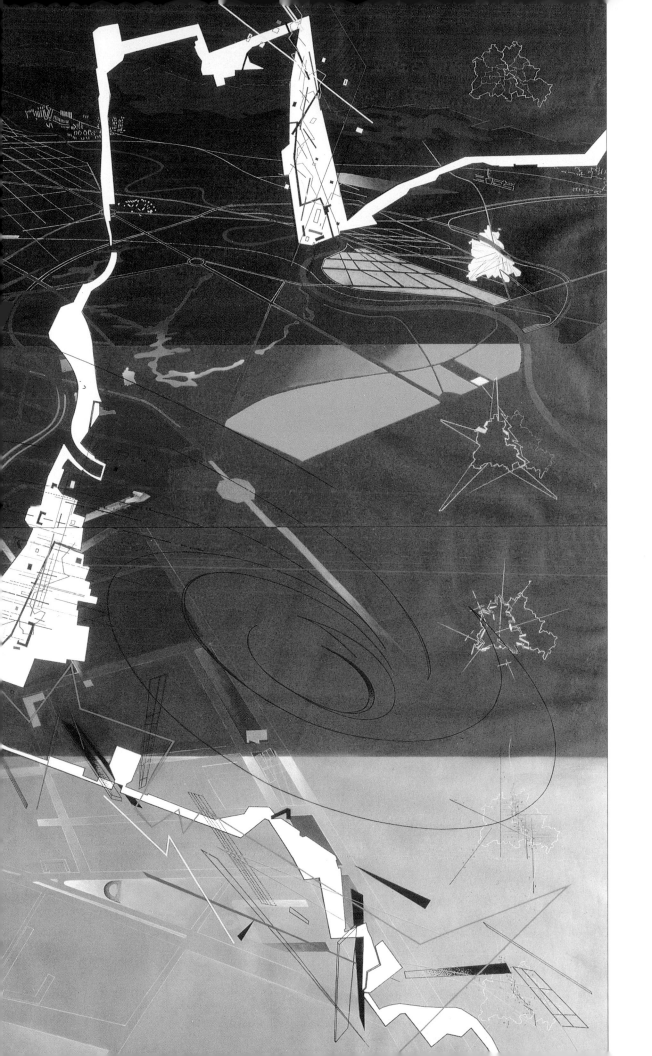

47

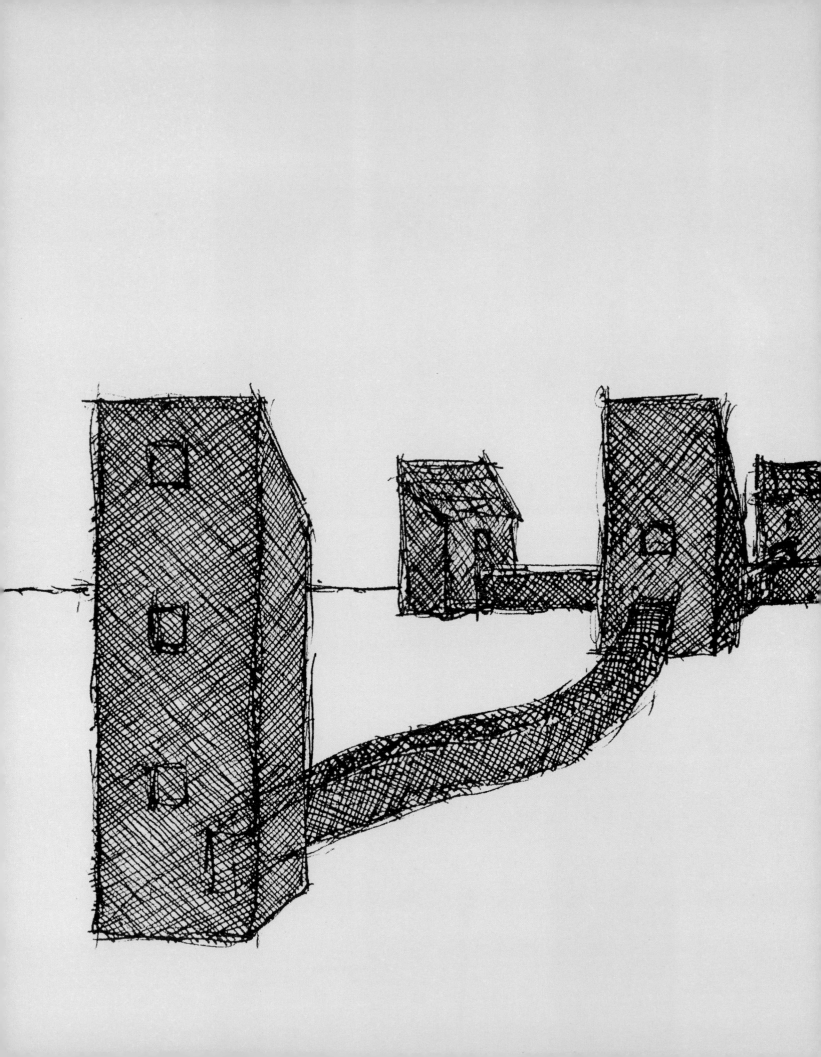

JOHN HEJDUK
THE POTSDAM PRINTER'S HOUSE/STUDIO

For the last four years I have been working on a major project called 'Berlin Night' and from this, I have submitted a single part entitled 'The Potsdam Printer's House/Studio'.

I have donated this work as a plea in opposition to super/master/grand/planning, which has destroyed so many significant places. I believe in the modest, incremental growth of cities. I am suspicious of grand schemes (they usually destroy the soul of place). I have therefore entered 'Potsdam Printer's House/Studio' in the hope that its scale and size might give a relative clue as to the particular atmospheres possible.

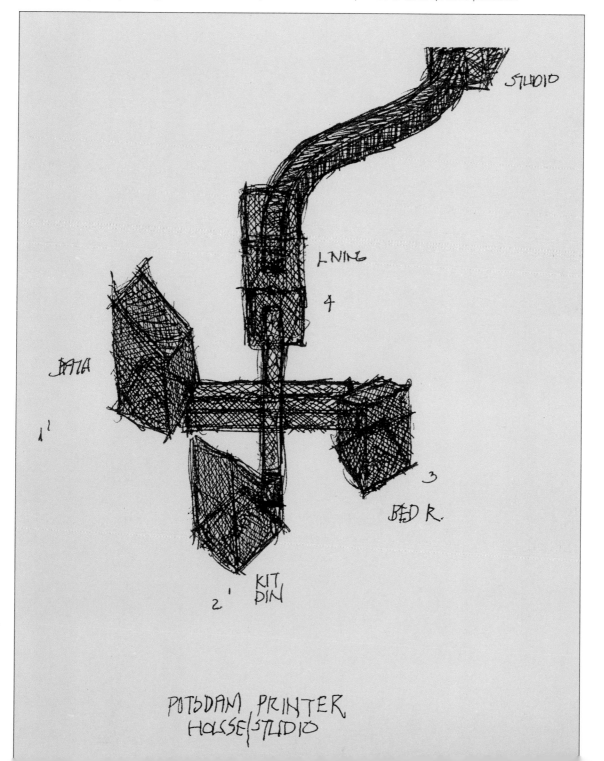

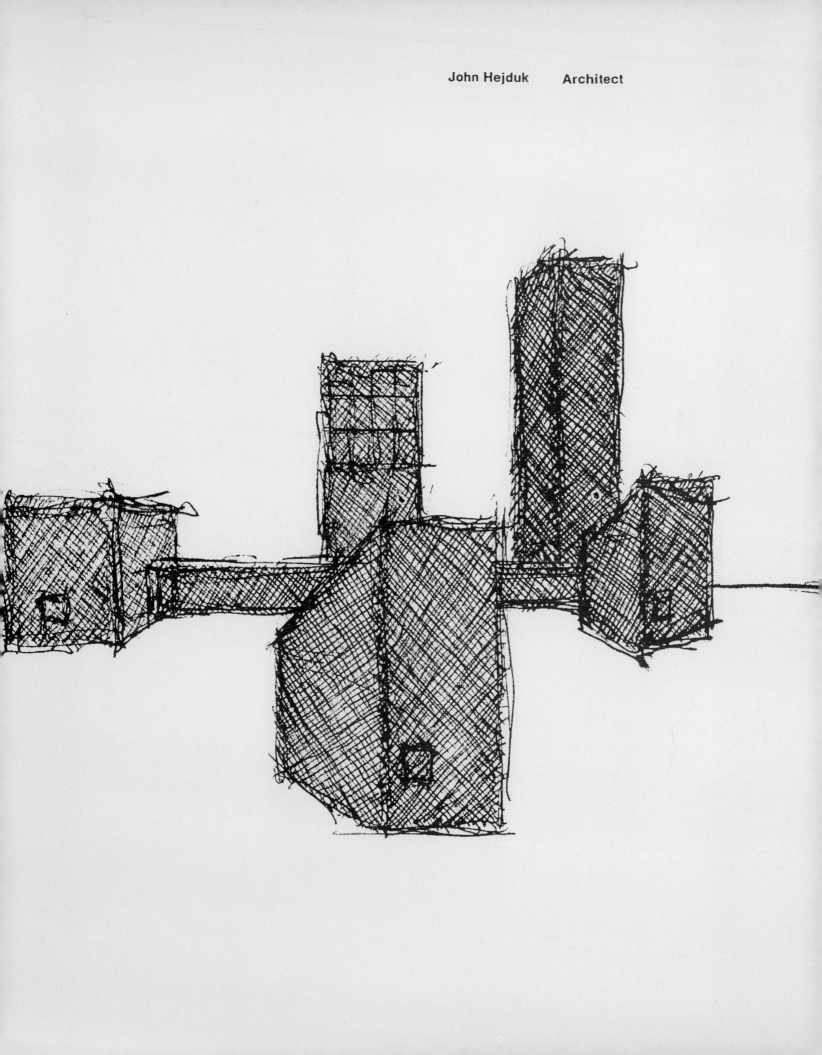

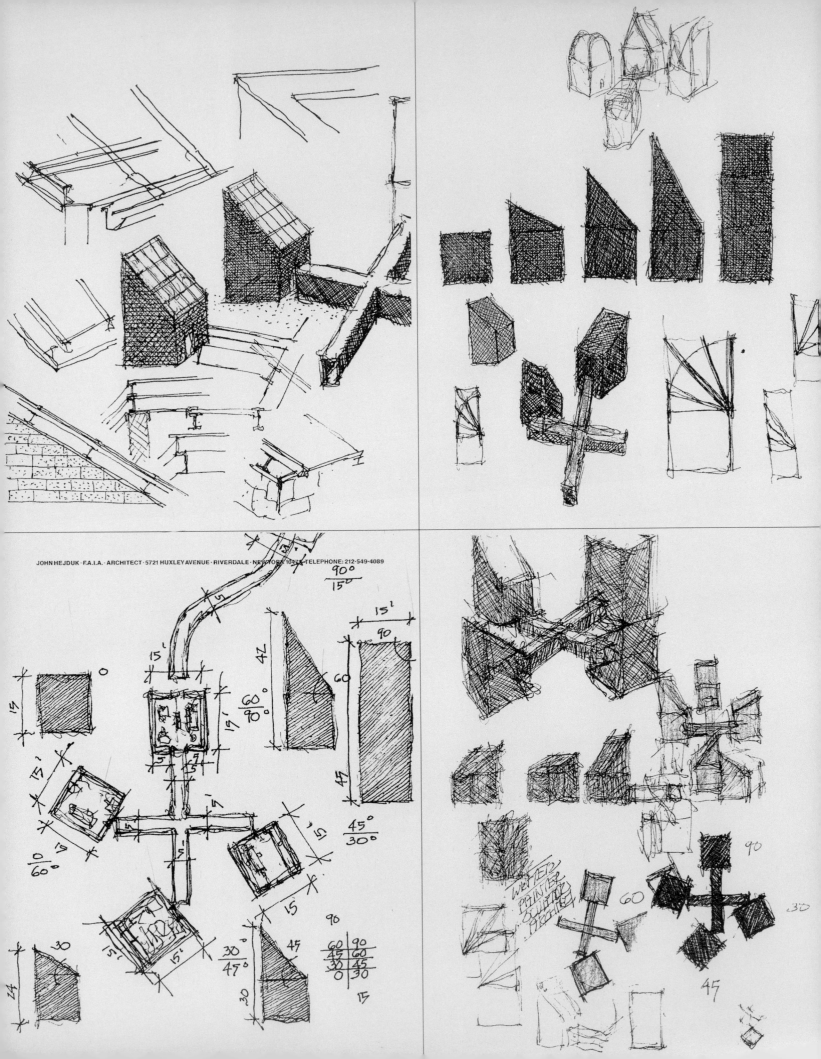

JOHN HEJDUK · F.A.I.A. · ARCHITECT · 5721 HUXLEY AVENUE · RIVERDALE · NEW YORK 10471 · TELEPHONE: 212-549-4089

JACQUES HERZOG, PIERRE DE MEURON & REMY ZAUGG
THE TIERGARTEN AS GEOMETRIC CENTRE

The Tiergarten is the geometric centre of Berlin's urban landscape. The lakes of Grosser Wannsee to the west and Grosser Müggelsee to the east reflect each other.

The form of the building is not the architectonic design given to it by the architect or artist. Nor is it the design which the economist or the technician or the structural engineer gives the building. It is the form which the observer gives the building.

The districts bordering on the Tiergarten are poorly linked. They are not bordered by the large expanse of green area, but cut off by it instead. The Tiergarten gives the impression of a space that happens to have been left empty and has not yet been developed.

Former traffic hubs and landmarks have been blocked by post-war urban development and have lost their former function: for example Leipziger/Potsdamer Platz by the construction of the Kulturforum.

Kurfürstendamm and Leipziger Strasse are to be linked to create a continuous axis. Together with the Strasse des 17 Juni and Unter den Linden, this will create a double axis linking the eastern and western areas of the city. The Kulturforum is to be regarded as part of the Tiergarten; isolated, free-standing buildings take the place of some existing marginal developments.

The specific character of the districts adjacent to Bahnhof Zoo railway station, Lützowplatz, Brandenburger Tor/Leipziger Platz and the Hamburger Güterbahnhof freight station is to be expressed in four buildings whose dimensions of scale, proportion and architectonic design distinguish them from the city's existing buildings. These four buildings create a spatial interrelationship that restructures the Tiergarten: the former space becomes an urban entity, an urban centre of Berlin's cityscape.

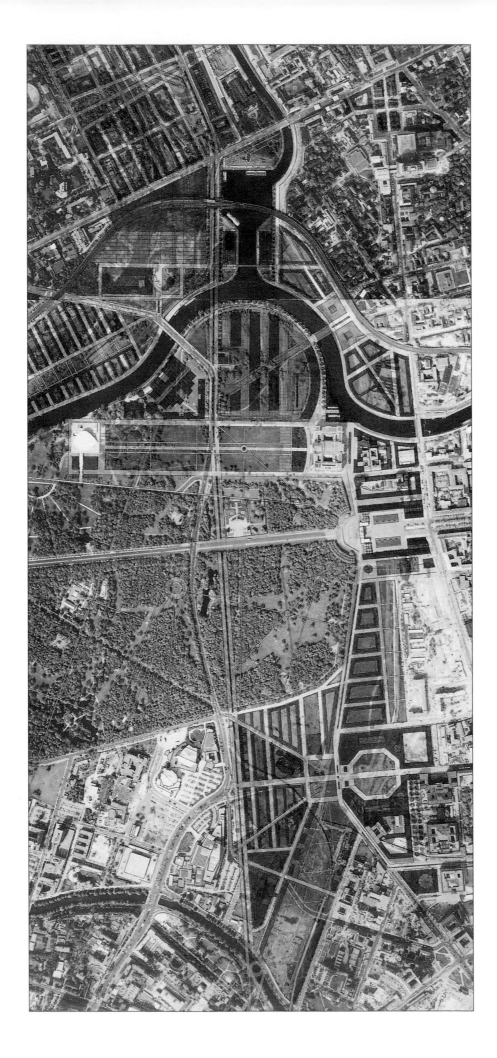

JOSEF PAUL KLEIHUES
INNOVATIVE URBAN MODELS NEED MASTERPLANS

The quality of life in a major city depends on a number of factors, not least of which is the degree of urban and architectural space it provides. This is an aim that should not be neglected in any part of a city.

Nevertheless, it is legitimate, in view of Berlin's future role as metropolis and future capital, to concentrate particular interest on the historic city centre and the so-called central area.

The 'central area' is defined as the area between the former railway station of Hamburger Bahnhof and the Yorck bridges, and it is this area which will be affected by the three fundamental town planning decisions that are to be reached in the coming weeks and months and which will be of historic significance for the urban function and quality of Berlin. These three fundamental decisions involve:

– determining the use and structure of the sweeping bend in the River Spree – the so-called 'Spreebogen' – as the future government quarter

– restructuring Potsdamer Platz and integrating the Mercedes Benz AG service centre and

– the realisation of the western thoroughfare.

The pragmatic brevity in which these fundamental decisions and the attached urban plan photocollage are justified here may prompt more complex considerations.

In view of Berlin's geographic situation in the united Europe of the future, the city cannot and must not fail to take the role of governmental capital. Was there not a tacit understanding that the Spreebogen should be reserved for a government district once the country was no longer divided? A segmented terrace could be built on this site for the house of parliament and several ministries.

The space in front of the Reichstag could be restructured to create an expansive modern urban area, acting as a gateway to the new government district while at the same time including the backdrop of the congress centre as a counterpoint to the Reichstag.

Nearby, Berlin's main railway station could be created at the rail intersection. The north-south line would have to be built underground in the central area.

Now that the Wall has finally come down, there is an opportunity of reconstructing the historic ground plan of Leipziger Platz and, at the same time, of revitalising Potsdamer Platz – not as a hub of communications, but as a magnificent urban space corresponding to the famous octagon of the Leipziger Platz.

It is admittedly painful that after 200 years of debate on the design of urban spaces to a unique triad of square, octagon and circle, this unparalleled opportunity should come to Potsdamer Platz only after the devastation of World War II and the demolition of Mendelsohn's Columbus Haus on 17th July 1956.

With the decision for Mercedes Benz AG to build a major service centre here, this opportunity has to be used prudently. It will be successful only if at least an equal volume of housing and facilities are built. The entire area between Tiergarten and Landwehrkanal covers some 200,000 square metres. About 80,000 square metres are required for streets and open spaces, green areas and facilities, leaving a net development site of 120,000 square metres. Even assuming a density of 5.0, five times 120,000 square metres of floor space could be created. That means 600,000 square metres, including the 240,000 square metres of the Mercedes Benz AG. This construction volume is desirable, indeed imperative, if a genuine piece of urban life is to be created here.

In Berlin, a cutback in road construction is both possible and desirable in many places. The construction of the western thoroughfare, at least in a united Berlin, is imperative from a functional and ecological point of view. Potsdamer Strasse has been unable to cope with the traffic crowding into Stresemannstrasse, Wilhelmstrasse and Friedrichstrasse. Not only could the flow of traffic break down completely, but also city centre housing streets and shopping streets could be blocked and would lose the atmosphere and quality of life they have so recently regained.

The western thoroughfare is not only indispensable as a bypass, but is also a fundamental requirement of urban development in the area of the railway junction (the so-called 'Gleisdreieck'), the area between Leipziger Platz and Kulturforum and the Spreebogen, or bend in the River Spree. This is based on the assumption that the western thoroughfare (in the form of a multi-lane boulevard) will be as straight as possible and able to accommodate east-west traffic from the streets running along the canal, the Strasse des 17 Juni and the Invalidenstrasse.

Aesthetic considerations also favour the construction of a major city boulevard with a six-metre wide green central reservation, and with cycle paths and double rows of trees on both sides.

No street in Berlin offers an urban experience over a length of three to four kilometres comparable to that which would be created by this western boulevard between the Yorck bridges and the bend in the River Spree, by cutting into the vast (and in future green) space of the former railway junction, bisecting the hopefully soon completed *Generalszug*, crossing the Landwehrkanal, Kulturforum, that links both city centres. After that comes the Tiergarten, the east-west axis with the Victory Column and Brandenburger Tor, Platz der Republik with the Reichstag and the Kongresshalle and, finally, the Spreebogen, the Spree and the Humboldthafen docks.

After years of destructive road-building, we dare not fall prey now to an urban antipathy born of an anti-technical Zeitgeist.

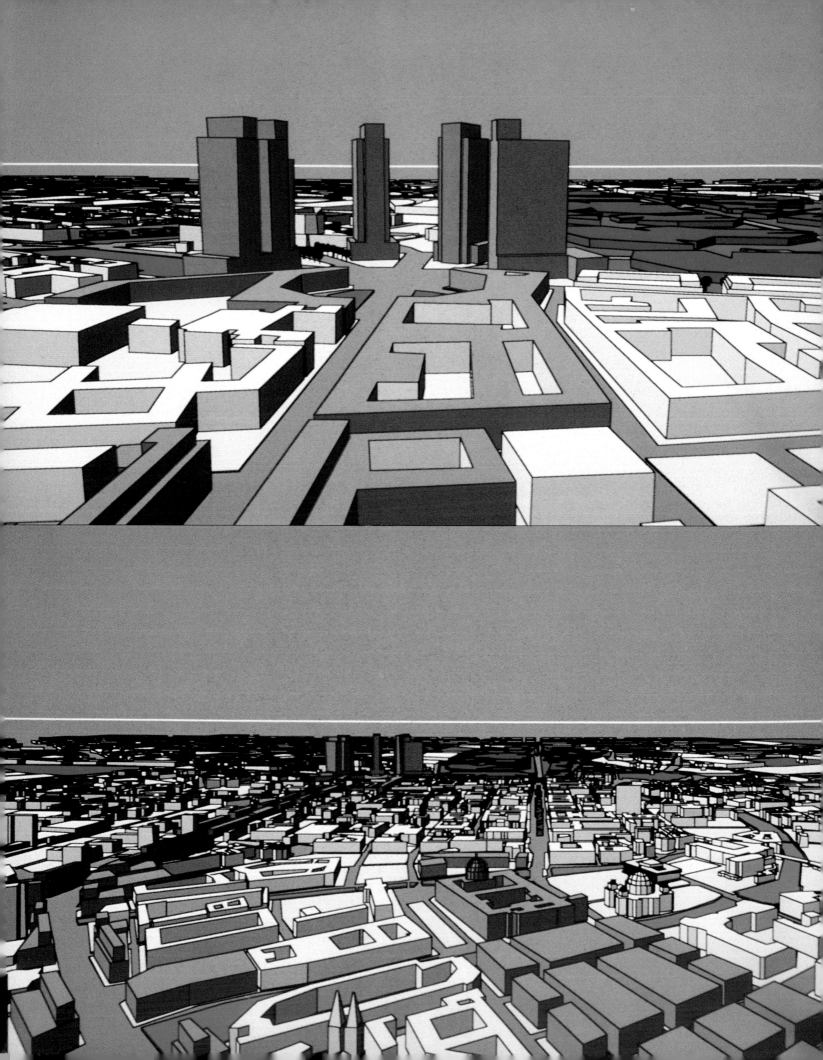

HANS KOLLHOFF
CITY LIMITS

If the Wall had any beneficial effect at all, it was in the way it contained the centrifugal forces of capitalistic urban expansion. At the moment, Berlin can count itself fortunate in comparison to any Western metropolis in having a virtually unscathed surrounding area – a unique situation indeed. In Berlin, it is still possible to take a trip into the countryside along magnificent tree-lined avenues. So let us draw the city limits tight and put a stop to anyone who, for their own convenience, wants to relegate everything that is too bulky to the outskirts.

Accordingly, because of their public transport links, Potsdamer Platz and Alexanderplatz will have to succumb to the pressure on service areas in the city, especially if they are to take some of the pressure off the historic centre. Both squares therefore have to be reconsidered in the light of their continued metropolitan *genius loci*.

This cannot be achieved without skyscrapers on an American scale, unless cosy provinciality is to be accepted from the Brandenburger Tor to the Gleisdreieck. What is meant here is that the sacred cow of Berlin planning – the maximum roof height – cannot be upheld in a development project that calls for verticality in order to make the most of the space available. Clinging to the regulation roof height means preventing skyscrapers from releasing their urban power; what could be generated on the street in terms of authentic urban atmosphere creates cancerous growths of the most undignified kind when relegated to the interior of a block. Anyone familiar with American skyscrapers knows that there, the entire structural volume, even if it is graduated and has the appearance of a socle edge, shoots up from the ground. There is a distinct main entrance through a spacious and carefully designed foyer that acts as a public space giving access to thousands of offices. Visitors are led to the lifts quite casually or can stroll through the mall-like foyer in which shops are accessible from inside and outside the building. On the ground floor, these skyscrapers differ very little from any properly functioning block in a major Western city.

Just as Alexanderplatz stretches its fingers towards the eastern districts, Potsdamer Platz looks to the western areas, albeit towards the emptiness of the Tiergarten. The Philharmonie, the Staatsbibliothek, the Nationalgalerie are like rings on the fingers of a hand. The historic city limits in the area of the former ministerial gardens are to be channelled towards the Tiergarten so that Potsdamer Platz can appear at the gates of the Baroque city as a conglomeration of six towers. Energies are concentrated here to restitute the historic proportions of Leipziger Platz on the one hand whilst keeping the site of the former Potsdamer Bahnhof railway station free for a city park. Each of the towers, with about 70 floors and a built-up area of 60 metres square, would have a gross floor space equivalent to that of the Chrysler Building – a floor space for which Daimler Benz wants to develop a 65,000 metre site. The 1.5 million square metres of gross floor area provided by the six towers corresponds to a site of some one million square metres – involving development of the entire area between Tiergarten and Landwehrkanal – that would otherwise be required if the old Berlin roof height regulation of 22 metres were to be maintained.

A high degree of efficiency is the prerequisite for maximum standards of architectural quality. In the public interest, Docklands standards cannot be accepted here. Perhaps the New York skyscrapers of the 30s or the Kontorhäuser in Hamburg could be taken as a yardstick to indicate the minimum standards Berlin has to aim for on this important site.

Collaboration: Norbert Hemprich.

64

DANIEL LIBESKIND
ÜBER DEN LINDEN

The future development of Berlin depends on the spirit of creative imagination whose substance is hope and whose proof is ethical conviction. This substance is faith in the city and its culture rather than the manipulation of economic/political variables for short-sighted gains under the cover of 'planning'. Exploration, not exploitation is paramount; invention, not calculation is necessary.

The project 'Über den Linden' seeks to substantiate the image of the historical centre of Berlin in scale, function and character through transformation of buildings, streets and former lines of division. To revitalise the historical East-West thoroughfare it is necessary to bring it into the dynamics of the 21st century both functionally and urbanistically. Only by breaking through the barriers of 19th-century planning and thought will the dam that held East separated from West (even before its political division) be breached, allowing the energies of Berlin to flood back freely into everyday life.

A new architecture is appropriate to the new Berlin. It is not by increasing income, while living on the same old capital and on the same stock of inherited architecture that Berlin can grow.

A radical, less certain and more vital enterprise is necessary, probing the depths of the spirit of Berlin from which its intellectual and social character takes sustenance. In this way an open architectural vision will become the reality of a new capital yielding new dividends and not just a 'one-time-sum' spent and forgotten.

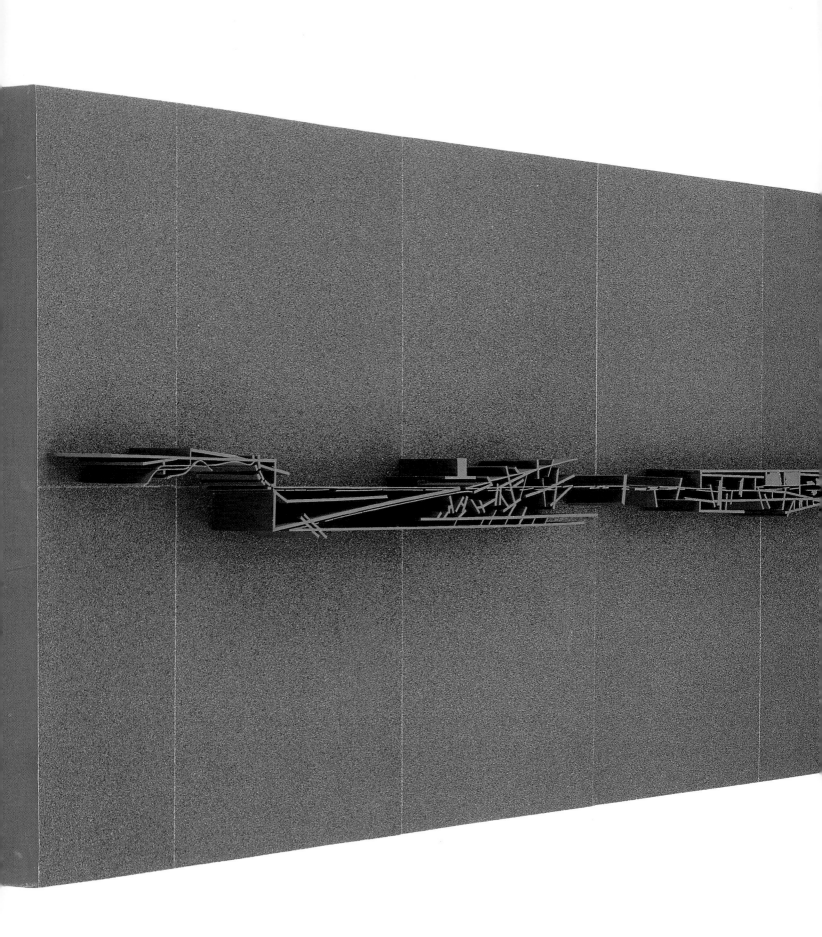

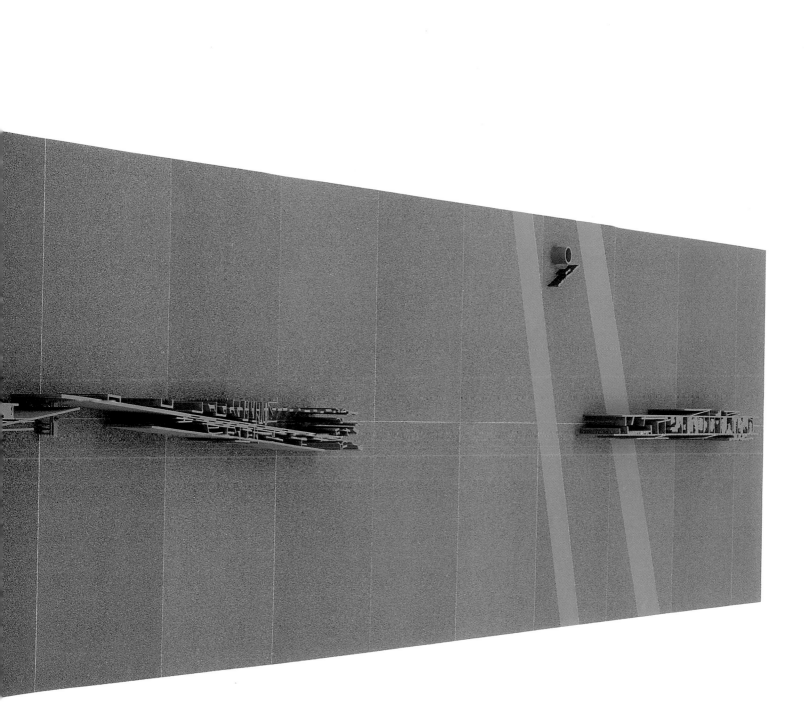

Ü B E

L I N

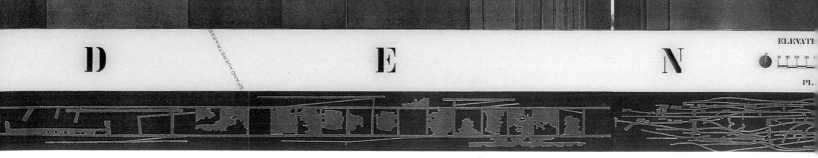

JEAN NOUVEL
THE MEETING LINE

In nearly three decades, the political schism of Germany has produced an entirely unique situation in Berlin. A completely different urban and architectural model has developed creating a dual city with two centres. Now that the Wall is down, hopefully this bipolarity will dissolve. However, it is unlikely that this will happen overnight. It will require a thoughtful approach and a slow path so that radical mistakes are not committed in the name of rapid progress. Political decisions could cause major changes in traffic patterns. Despite these potential changes, we have formulated a number of hypothetical situations to lay the framework for our proposition. It seems likely that the main political institutions will be located along a loose axis running from Brandenburger Tor to Alexanderplatz. Secondly, a cultural promenade could be imagined running from the forum to the museum complex near the Dom. The Friedrichstrasse is likely to become a major business and commercial axis.

As for the canyon that was once the Wall, we see a major opportunity to create a new core for public animation day and night. The lobotomy and mummification of space that has played such a tragic role in the life of the city now seems irrelevant. Its transformation into a place of renewed life will symbolise the hope and optimism of the Berliners.

Friedrichstrasse: light it up, colour it, enlarge it, deepen your visions. It would be irrelevant to laboriously fill the voids. It seems more sensible to use (and abuse) the characteristic anomalies and surprises.

The anomalies: empty lots on each side of the street, squares in progress, more remnant than deliberate; large walls, blind and sad; bridges for the S-Station and Checkpoint Charlie.

The surprises: perspectives at the end of crossing streets; needles and domes emerging above and between buildings.

Propositions: to make public the spaces on both sides of the street and to express the ground forcefully by way of dotting, painting, informing, lighting, bordering, lining; to light up every empty wall with narrow 'billboard-buildings' so that Friedrichstrasse will be bathed with light, colours and the logos of the firms which occupy it; to animate the bridges of the Station and Checkpoint Charlie with digitilised light-news and electronic billboards; to create in the perspectives between buildings additional emerging objects, totems, new symbols for public buildings and corporate firms. To suggest a deeper field of vision and consciousness of the metropolis.

The Meeting Line: to mark the end of a situation which was considered fatal, to reinforce the desire that these horrors should never repeat themselves and to eradicate the existence of a No Man's Land under constant surveillance from watch towers, I propose to create along this long scar, a 'meeting line'. This will be crossed by a series of streets, long closed and new. A sinuous space, a sort of golf green, shining with small optimistic lights and coloured like the crossing of a golf course with a computer grid. Along this ribbon, different sequences will take place linked by covered walkways for families, joggers, cyclists, young lovers. There will be lively spaces devoted to shoppers, meditators, peeping toms – all the good and bad crazies of the metropolis; also a series of spaces equipped with shops, bars, restaurants and night-clubs, flower shops, book shops, candy stores and bike stores – images of life. There will be housing and office buildings along the way, offering great views. Thus the city will dare to look at itself again and smile in its new mirror and at its new reality.

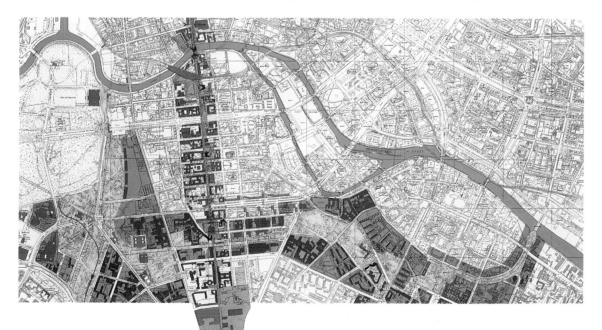

Die Meeting Line

Leuchtschriftfassaden

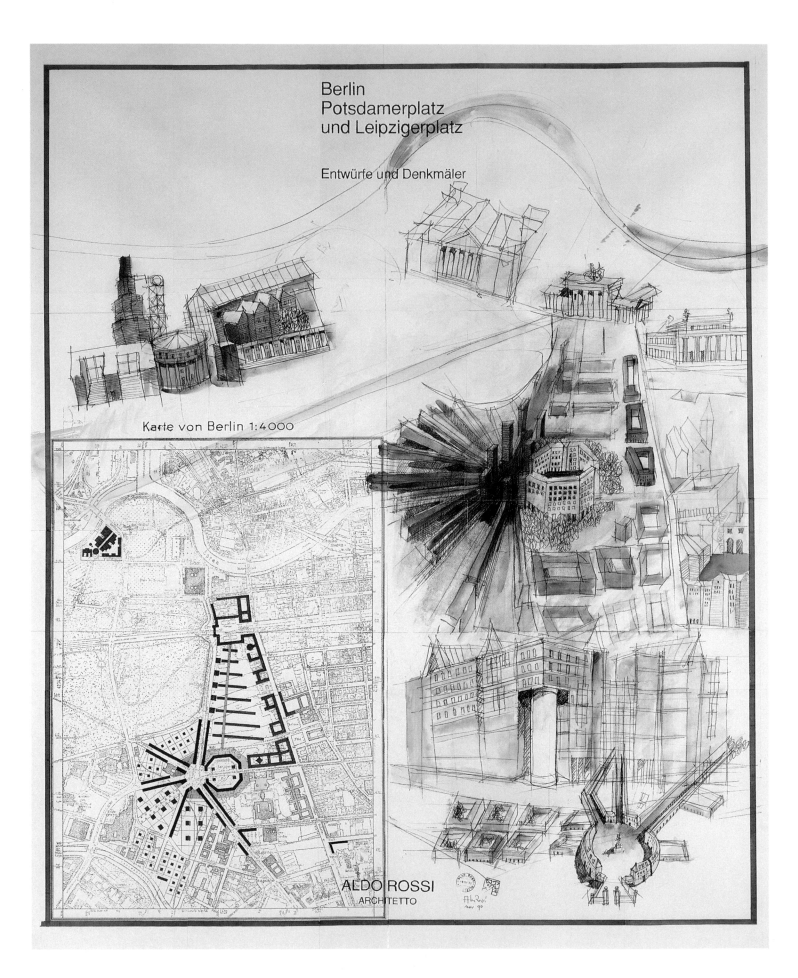

Berlin
Potsdamerplatz
und Leipzigerplatz

Entwürfe und Denkmäler

Karte von Berlin 1:4000

ALDO ROSSI
ARCHITETTO

ALDO ROSSI

POTSDAMER PLATZ AND LEIPZIGER PLATZ

Berlin is a unique and singularly beautiful city; so unique, indeed, that its division by a wall for an entire generation did not even seem particularly odd. Perhaps no other city in the world could have managed to integrate such a 'Wall' in its history. To find one, we would have to return to the mythical cities of the orient, to urban settlements whose meaning has been lost to us. After all, the 'Wall' was something mythical in our eyes and will remain so in our memories.

Berlin has a singular beauty; singular because it is so inextricably linked with the city's destiny. As a city that was built abstractly, attracting many peoples as it grew, proud of its ominous power, a city that has known destruction, division, reconstruction, Berlin has always exuded a certain fascination.

This also explains the fascination of its architecture: the workers' districts and the woods, the settlements of the 'Neues Bauen' period and the monuments of the Nazi era, the Stalinallee, the Nationalgalerie by Mies van der Rohe, the columns by Schinkel that traverse the German forest.

Just as any German architect would go on an 'Italian Journey', as a student, I wandered through Berlin. Nobody could ever convince me that *one* architecture or *one* form could be right for this city.

That is why I accepted the challenge posed by the Deutsches Architektur-Museum and the *Frankfurter Allgemeine Zeitung*. I do not wish to call it a competition or a proposal or even a concept, because I do not believe that it will have tangible consequences. However, it does express alternative ideas for Berlin and alternative statements about this city, as was already the case in the competition for the Alexanderplatz and other projects.

I also accepted it because of the openness that great capital cities have always shown towards architects from other countries.

It is like seeing the skyline of a city on an exceptionally clear evening, recognising the monuments and houses; it is like catching a fleeting glimpse of those familiar or imaginary places that appear only on those splendidly lucid evenings when the architecture is merely the visible or tangible expression of destiny and all that is colourless, superfluous or simply distracting disappears with the setting sun.

There is a beautiful wartime photo of the Brandenburger Tor and the dried-out trees on the avenue of Unter den Linden. Perhaps that is the only meaning of the drawing in which images gathered on walls through the city come together. Leipziger Platz has become a monument that is reminiscent of the Belle-Alliance-Platz almost exactly as we know it from old etchings; appropriately for its architecture, it stands alone as though there were nothing around it, yet at the same time enriched by the French language. Linked to the Leipziger Platz is Potsdamer Platz – the hub, the watershed and the point of bisection of the long streets that cross the city and even continue beyond into the countryside, Prussia, the eastern plains. Like the roads the Romans built, like the roads of Vauban, they were built for a different purpose, for a function without frontiers, not as the streets of a city.

And the city? Whether it is encircled by a wall or divided by a wall, it is reorganised in its parts. As we said before: plans and monuments; because there cannot be *one* plan and *one* monument, but only an attempt at interpreting the destiny of the city.

DENISE SCOTT BROWN & ROBERT VENTURI
BERLIN WHEN THE WALL COMES DOWN

THE WALL: *We are not Berliners, but we have tried to enter into the new Berlin by carefully examining the documents you have sent us, using our heads and eyes but mainly our hearts. From Philadelphia, we cannot design buildings for Berlin but we can suggest ways of thinking about change in the city, now the wall is removed. Understanding the forces for change should help architects evolve a new Berlin architecture that both reweaves the urban fabric and points the way to the future.*

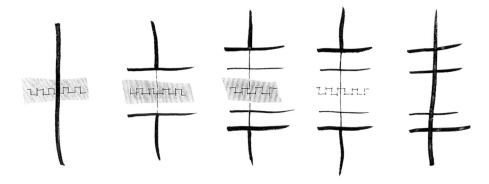

What happens to a road when it is blocked off?
At first there is silence. The traffic diverts and goes about its business within its own sector. Crossroads become busier; approaching the barrier, traffic volume slowly decreases until the last sections have little or no traffic. The street acquires a sadly deserted air. If it was once a broad and busy main street lined with proud buildings, the few cars on it and the disrepair of its surfaces give it a haunted atmosphere, which intensifies when buildings are cleared around the barrier.

Then when the road is reopened?
Now the traffic can flow again, but a new set of connections has been formed; we will never go back to the old city.

What should be done when the Wall comes down?
We don't know, but commercial and governmental interests are poised to bring about further change; the intentions of the transportation engineers should be watched as carefully as those of the developers. Walls have come down in Berlin before and in each case, new arrangements of the urban infrastructure and new patterns of use have resulted. In order to help Berlin establish a new unity, we must understand the city's growth and development from its start, because traces of that start and of the city's subsequent history are literally in the ground that we are considering. Because we are looking at maps and photographs, not the reality, we can derive the history in only very general ways and we will certainly be wrong in some ways; you will have to correct us.

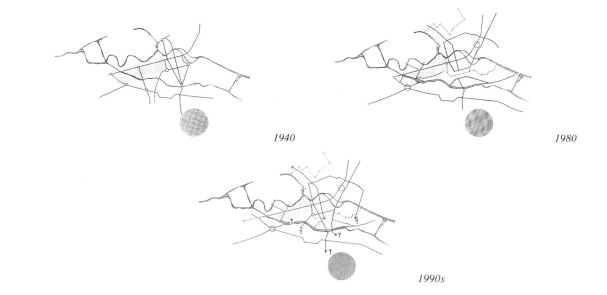

1940

1980

1990s

READING HISTORY FROM THE MAP

Berlin was first a safe spot by a river near a large marsh. The city grew beyond a series of walls that were sequentially removed.

Eventually, the city grew beyond all walls, marshland was drained, major open spaces were laid out and a Burgher city was developed. This mercantile city spread to the west. Unter den Linden was already the site of proud institutions.

With industrialisation, a pretzel of rail lines was built to encircle the city east and west of the Spree. Passengers arrived at several terminals at the rim of the centre of town, and the build-up of Berlin as a mass city took place. More institutions were set along Unter den Linden west of the Spree, and the commercial heart of the city was north and south of these.

As the 19th century became the 20th century, so street car lines were added, and what Americans call 'street car suburbs' developed west and south of the centre. Here the population could live at a density that was urban but not intense. At the centre of this new city, commercial expansion was blocked by the Tiergarten, so it slipped to the southwest and headed towards the Breitscheid Platz, which became a retail centre for the residential areas around it. During the 1930s, an airport near the centre of Berlin was initiated. It is one of the few large city airports that are almost in town.

Only by knowing the shape of this pre-war city can one understand what has happened in Berlin since, first through the bombing, then through the Wall and the different attitudes taken towards urban renewal west and east of it.

Bombs cut a swathe through Berlin from east to west, sparing some of the grandeur of the Unter den Linden, but peppering the centre extensively and wiping out the area south of the Tiergarten – though some of what looks like bombing may in fact have been post-war clearance for urban renewal.

With the post-war political stand-off and the Wall, Berlin became a symbol of the Cold War. Each side saw the rebuilding of the city as a showcase to the other. The two systems stand clearly depicted in their plans for Berlin. The capitalist city massed its commercial and financial activities along the Kurfürstendamm. To the east, socialist planning was demonstrated in housing on the Stalinallee and in the redesigns of the great urban places destroyed by bombs. Commerce and retail, evident as a structuring element of West Berlin, appear in the east to be subsumed within governmental and administrative buildings. At the local level, retail in the east is related to housing enclaves, along with kindergartens and other community facilities, in a cellular pattern visible on the map.

The two town centres drew away from each other – one from Alexanderplatz towards the Stalinallee, the other west down the Kurfürstendamm, taking its hold from the remains of pre-war commercial activities around Breitscheid Platz. These redirections were supported by the realignment and replacement of roads, the location of housing, the use of the airport, and even the use of the transit system. These vast changes took place primarily through the adaptation of what remained of the historic urban patterns.

What will happen now the Wall is gone?

Will East Berliners move across the city everyday to jobs in the west? Will outposts of the western economy be formed in the eastern sector to employ people living there? The answers to such questions may lie only partly in policy; this is not a plea for further city planning – it is, rather, that we consider the likely effects of city physics.

Medieval Berlin: The Walled City

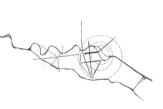

The Burgher City

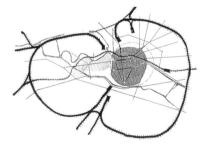

The Railroad City

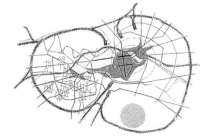

The Street-Car City

The Capitalist and Socialist Cities

CITY PHYSICS
The Urban Stress Diagram

Over its history, Berlin has grown as a set of patterns on patterns. At any one time, this inherited infrastructure has been differentially weighted, to accord with different uses of sectors within the city. The road and rail systems form a stress diagram, whose vectors change according to changes in the intensity of use of sectors of the city, and also changes in the means of making connections between them.

The removal of the Wall will give rise to changes in population movement, the daily journey to work, street configurations, development patterns and urban infrastructure. These will vastly redistribute the pattern of stresses on the city. Even the reopening of stops in the subway system as well as the new accessibility of the present airport to East Berlin will produce new pressures. Where new roads are placed, where new airports and other transit facilities are introduced, further pressures will occur.

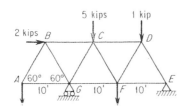

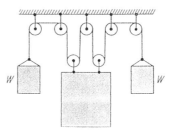

Where are the most precious and vulnerable parts of the city?

These may not be the places to introduce intense new development; particularly new road alignments or rail and transit changes, because they increase accessibility and may induce pressures for change beyond what is desirable.

Visionaries for Berlin today must also be good 'physicists' who understand how the urban stress diagram is likely to shift. They must think ahead of the implications of actions government and citizens are likely to take. All changes will bring pressure on the urban tissue, some welcome and some not. At times, it will be possible to go with the forces, channelling them in directions believed to be desirable for the city. At times, it may be necessary to stand against the forces. But this will require a good knowledge of how city systems work. To make water run uphill, you must be an excellent engineer – and you can't do it too often.

To understand the new stress diagram for Berlin, visionary architects should set out the city's hot and cold spots (places where change is likely and not likely), and hard and soft spots (places where change would be difficult or should not happen, and places where it could be invited and would be easy). A map of both patterns overlaid on one sheet would be very interesting, even for city politicians.

From inspection of maps, we think that the Unter den Linden is a hard area where large-scale change would be hurtful and should be resisted. Directly south is, we suspect, an area vulnerable to change, especially from growth around the airport and between the Potsdamer

Platz and Checkpoint Charlie. Is it a precious historic area that should not be changed, or should it grow incrementally by small-scale changes? The area south of the Tiergarten between the Wall and the Kurfürstendamm appears to be suitable for large-scale change; it could be important to the re-establishment of connections between west and east.

Given the new stress diagram, architects should ask where will retail uses go in a reunited Berlin? Can the face-to-face contact of the small office workplace and the coffee shop be introduced to the monumentality of the public sector in the east? Where do the artists go? (Artists are urban scouts; they find good places in the city that have not been discovered; they induce cycles of development – from artists to young architects to young lawyers to the rest of us. Then the artists move on.) Where do the artists go, east and west? (Remember, this means 'where are they likely to want and afford to go?', not 'where will we put them?') Where do poor people go?

This is not city planning but city physics

It owes little to the grand ideas of the Kaiser, the Nazis, or Le Corbusier, but, rather, to the reasoning of Von Thunen, Kristaller and Losch. Yet, it is not a supine resignation to *laissez-faire*. We've grown it from the maps alone; we may be wrong, but we have tried to suggest a way of thinking. Your policies (or your principled lack of them) must reckon with city physics, as builders of Berlin have done, working with or against the forces, throughout history.

Urban Stress Diagram

'Hard Places' and 'Hot Spots'

NEW THREADS IN AN OLD WEB
Can an east-west link be made?

We cannot make plans sitting in Philadelphia but, again, entering the maps we have tried to make suggestions at several scales.

Visionary architects should want a city that combines the best of the West and East, and underplays the less desirable aspects of each; that builds on what has been, even as it pushes the capitalist and socialist cities, within the wall, into the category of history, considering them as part of an earlier inherited pattern.

Think of how the change in terms of pressure points that will be developed at first through re-establishing the old connections, and then from the new dynamic that will result once the reconnections are made. Consider, for example, the new accessibility of East Berlin to the airport, or the effect of reopening closed stops on the underground, or of the effect of making new connections between rail lines and rail terminals, or of rerouting buses, and, particularly, of new building by government and the private sector.

This thinking should set a broad framework for analysis and design of areas within the system.

South of the Tiergarten

As a bold step in reknitting the fabric of Berlin, we suggest linking the Kurfürstendamm with the Alexanderplatz via a grand avenue along the south edge of the Tiergarten. The new connection would provide not only a physical link, but also a civic artery steeped in historical significance.

Curving north towards the Brandenburg Gate and Unter den Linden, the avenue should acknowledge the ghost of Potsdamer and Leipziger platz while integrating with the older Berlin of cultural, institutional and civic importance.

The avenue should be lined by buildings that look onto the park. It should be an auspicious route for cars and buses. Its sidewalks should be wide enough for strolling. Off the road between the civic and institutional buildings that exist in this area, should be enclaves of five to seven- storey buildings, traditional in many European cities. The buildings should be mainly residential with associated retail and community services. Although this was probably a commercial area before the war, we feel it unnecessary that the former dense city uses be replaced; rather the new buildings should be like the Nash terraces and crescents around Regent's Park in London. This planning approach would re-establish a continuity and create a bridge among various architectural spaces, historical and political eras and functional zones. The new Tiergarten Boulevard area would symbolically acknowledge evolution, communication and variety within the city and with its dynamic past. By reinforcing a linear connection it would enhance the sense of the whole and would ultimately define a new integration with a united Berlin.

There would be alternatives with potential for amenity at both lower and higher densities than the one suggested, and also a potential for a mixture of higher and lower buildings. We think there should be higher, denser buildings, particularly hotels, where this neighbourhood joins Kurfürstendamm and the Brandenburg Gate. In all cases, the existing infrastructure of facilities should be carefully associated with the housing, which in turn should be related to the park.

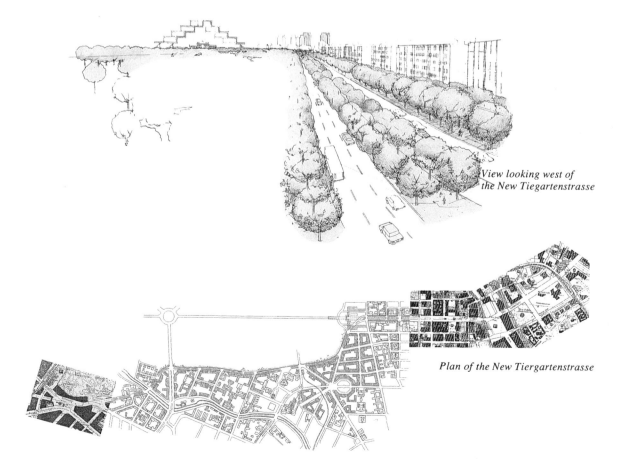

*View looking west of
the New Tiergartenstrasse*

Plan of the New Tiergartenstrasse

THE PUBLIC BERLIN
Berlin's Public Spine

Removing the Wall at the Brandenburg Gate will reunite the spine of parks and institutions that run from the Tiergarten in the west, through the Brandenburg Gate, to the Unter den Linden and beyond to the Stalinallee. These were the fame of pre-war Berlin.

The main axis through the Tiergarten is probably safe from destruction owing to its location, but the fate of the Unter den Linden is less assured. Through whatever forces of history, this is one of the few, perhaps the only, institutional streets in Europe that does not have a major commercial component. We feel strongly it should remain that way.

The identity of the Alexander and Marx-Engels Platz will change with the union between east and west. How this change will or should be undertaken is not for us to say. It should involve a debate between the city of Berlin and the German Republic. In many cities, there are governmental centres that contain no retail uses, but these are seldom near residential areas, as they are in East Berlin. Here we feel the face-to-face contact of people across a square should involve more than governmental interaction. Should the fringes of these squares, or indeed portions of their internal spaces, be given over to small offices and shops?

Whatever the nature of the changes, architects should consider the link between the Alexanderplatz and the Unter den Linden, across the island of the Spree. Here, a shift in axis occurs on the site that holds a parking lot and the Volkskammer. What uses and structures could make a great link between a governmental and perhaps national centre and a series of world institutions on the Unter den Linden? The connection between the Marx-Engels Platz and the Stalinallee, at the other end, is almost as important.

The Spree Ufer

The banks of the River Spree, the areas of the city assigned to our firm, are extremely important parts within the whole, but we feel they should be designed over a longer period of time than that available to us, in collaboration with local communities, and after a careful analysis of uses along them. Inspired responses, in this case, must derive from specific circumstances.

Here, we can only say be pragmatic; be sensitive and specific towards the variety that is there in order to make this linear zone agreeable and a lively foil to the other, more symbolically-formed and civically-scaled parts of the city.

The wonderful qualities of the winding river are precious and should be preserved. The Spree edges have been hardened over the centuries by engineers and architects into smooth curves and steep embankments. Notice the lively play of the decoration of balustrades and bridges against the heavy embankment. Between them, these define both community and individual. What would be an expression of both on the Spree today?

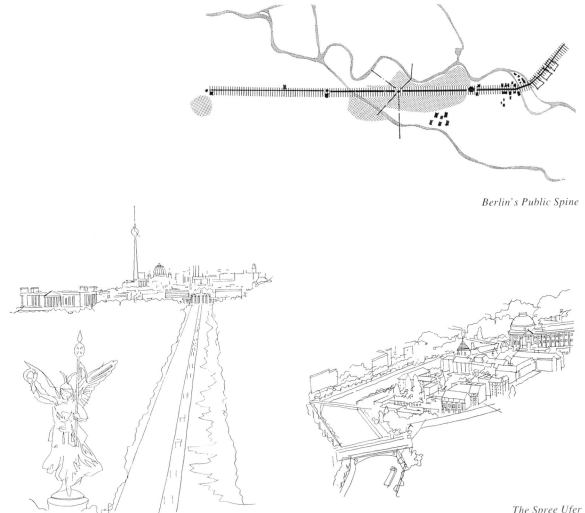

Berlin's Public Spine

Strasse des 17 Juni

The Spree Ufer

BRANDENBURG STAIR

This is perhaps the most symbolic location for the removal of the Wall. Potsdamer and Leipziger Platz offer more opportunity for resurgence through architecture, and Checkpoint Charlie has other symbolic meanings, but the Brandenburg Gate is the prime symbol. Here where no building should be, we have recommended a second gateway to the east and west. The structure itself is raised above eye level to permit the Brandenburg Gate to maintain its own spiritual and symbolic function. The new arch links old and new as well as east and west.

The symbol expresses bridging, coming together via climbing to higher levels of understanding and tolerance, and a surmounting of problems that had seemed intractable. It spans across the Brandenburg Gate and reinforces the passage through, at pedestrian level, and over, at a higher gestural level. It is a grand civic gesture like the Eiffel Tower, the St Louis Arch or the Washington Monument, but unlike those late 19th and mid-20th century structures, this bridge-as-stairs acts more explicitly as a civic symbol. A structural *tour de force* rather than an elegant structural gesture, the bridge is an immediate, memorable image – explicit, joyous, and beautiful.

Collaboration: David Schaaf, Nancy Rogo Trainer, Steven Wiesenthal.

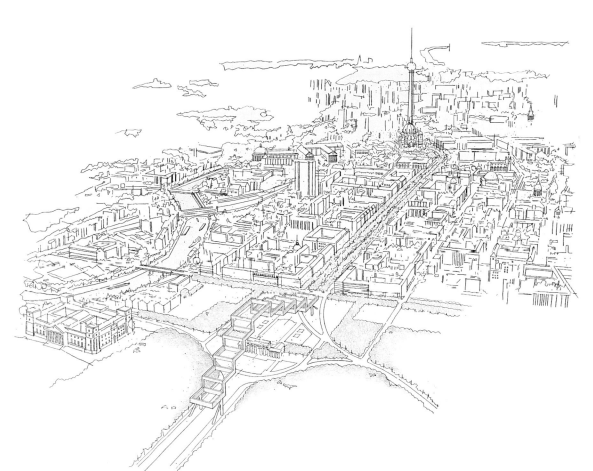

The Brandenburg Stair

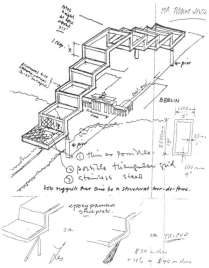

Structural Engineer Sketch

MANUEL DE SOLÀ-MORALES
THE ABSTRACT CITY

Berlin is a city defined by distances; a city in which the recurrence and sequence of the buildings counts for less than the recurrence and sequence of the spaces between them. It is this abstract pattern of long, drawn-out empty spaces that has shaped the urban grid. In contrast to the density and coherence of urban development in West Berlin, socialist East Berlin has not been heavily developed, priority being given to widely spaced inner-city housing blocks on the one hand and the symbolic buildings of the city centre on the other. The urban structure of East Berlin thus appears as an exercise in keeping things apart, as a spatial separation of buildings according to various different activities and purposes.

In East Berlin, plans must take into account the sense of community which has arisen from a mutual perception of the city as a place that brings people together. This tradition should be respected by avoiding over-zealous development, particularly of sites in the city centre. Above all, care must be taken to prevent the kind of unnecessary planning and development errors that have been made and legitimised on purely technocratic or ideological grounds. The problems posed by the centre of Berlin are essentially those of the constant East-West conflict. This is reflected in every aspect of the city's urban structure since its origins. From Old Berlin and Friedrichstadt to Charlottenburg, Potsdam and Brandenburg, history is manifest – counterbalanced only in the construction of the Karl-Marx-Allee.

The Kurfürstendamm extends to Alexanderplatz

Berlin's central axis could be based on a treble East-West link in future. First, a historic and currently recognised central axis of monumental and representative character: Prenzlauer Allee – Karl-Liebknecht-Strasse – Unter den Linden – Strasse des 17 Juni. A second axis constituting a strong backbone which still lacks appeal, but is almost complete: Greifswalder Strasse – Grunerstrasse – Gertraudenstrasse – Leipziger Strasse – Potsdamer Strasse. The third axis: a new, central thoroughfare extending the Kurfürstendamm to the old part of Berlin by restructuring existing streets, linking the area around Am Zoo, Tiergarten Strasse, Kulturforum, Akademieplatz, Kongress and Rathaus, and culminating in Alexanderplatz. This new link would create a central shopping and entertainment boulevard par excellence: a street for strolling, with pavement cafes, galleries, theatres, shops and advertising. This would give the Kulturforum a new urban context and the areas around Friedrichstadt would gain new points of reference both eastwards and westwards. A link between the Kurfürstendamm and Alexanderplatz would represent the unification of two different urban centres. This project would require some new architecture to lend it more emphatic urban definition: a building with a special facade looking onto

Kemper Platz, bringing life to the Kulturforum and stretching out into the green area of the Tiergarten park; furthermore, buildings would transform the Rathausstrasse into a bustling shopping street and the currently empty green area could be made into a playground, sports field, park and promenade. The buildings should be of medium height, publicly owned, and free of advertising, with certain premises specifically earmarked as ateliers for the use of artists, others for the use of students and university staff. Along the extended Tiergartenstrasse, between Wilhelmstrasse, Ebertstrasse, Pariser Platz and Potsdamer Platz, a new complex of housing, offices, hotels and theatres would be built to form a modern centre for the city of today. Far from symbolically exaggerating the memory of the wall, this new district should, in its everyday life and its various activities and facilities, reflect the definitive unification of the two Berlins. In our proposal, Alexanderplatz forms the beginning (or the end) of the new Kurfürstendamm. We envisage this square as a major hub of public transport and a focal point for traffic and pedestrians. In the interests of a more distinctive urban definition of this central area, Karl-Marx-Allee and Alexanderstrasse are to be restructured to create a more intensive interaction of buildings and streets, public spaces, traffic and pedestrians. This new structure should visually complement the existing high-rise buildings, placing the pavements, walkways and open spaces in a new perspective.

The Volksplatz

In this part of our project, we propose a complex of buildings, arranged and designed to complement existing elements which characterise the rebuilt western part of the city: very wide streets, isolated blocks of facades, generous open spaces and housing being the dominant features. Full use should be made of these urban elements in a clearly defined layout of such formal density that the centre of the Volksstadt takes on a distinctly recognisable character. This would create a collective urban area within the city, reflected in the infrastructure of the public transport and consumer facilities as well as in the fact that central sites cannot fall into private ownership – as, for example, in Galata, Istanbul or Times Square, New York. This new area is to be created as a roofed structure over the street intersection. Driving along Grunerstrasse, the 40-metre columns and the large flat roof spanning this newly planned central area like a huge open market can be seen from a distance. Starting with the renovated 'Haus des Lehrers', this urban renewal would alter the scale of interpretation of existing buildings and public squares; the city centre is defined by a conglomeration of blocks of housing, hotels and department stores lining the streets. This huge, open, columned hall contains metro access points and provides a public forum where large numbers of people can gather for demonstrations and political events – as in the outer courts of the medieval cathedrals, thus embodying the tradition of a 'People's Meeting Place', both open and covered.

The apartment tower blocks embrace the most modern concepts of experimental urban housing: they consist of apartments for young people, ie high-density transitional quarters with working and leisure areas. Construction would be state subsidised – a system already tested elsewhere. The existing 'stadt Berlin' hotel building forms the focal point of the 'peninsula' created by the new buildings, paying homage to the former socialist city with its impressive Karl-Marx-Allee.

All our proposals and ideas are based on an upbeat concept of the city as an interwoven complex of spaces and sequences. We wish to add to this interwoven structure without escapism and without nostalgia, following the example of a city whose empty spaces, in their sheer density, have become a rich and abstract element of the *forma urbis* in a manner unparalleled elsewhere.

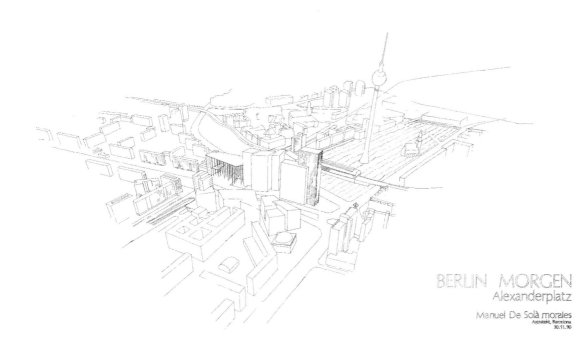

BERLIN MORGEN
Alexanderplatz

Manuel De Solà morales
Architekt, Barcelona
30.11.90

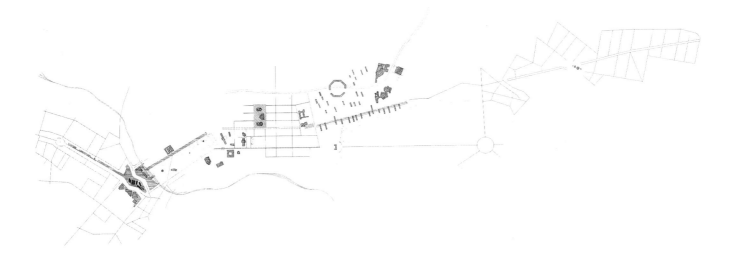

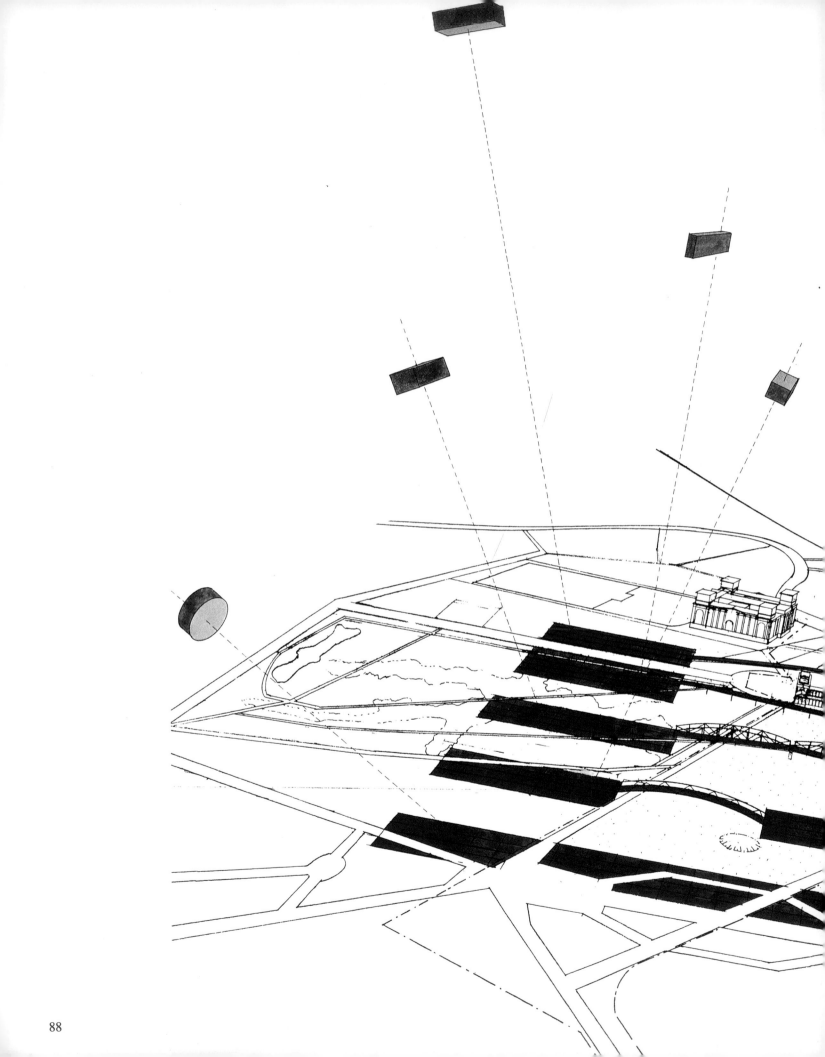

BERNARD TSCHUMI
EASTERN BLOCKS

Cities expand and contract. Berlin at the end of this century might expand again. Instead of expanding West Berlin into East Berlin, we propose to expand the East Berlin block structure over the traces of the wall (between Brandenburger Tor and Alexander Platz) into Tiergarten. Such a block structure would turn into a set of platforms and bridges that would act as the generator of new urban spectacles: fairs, theatres, exhibitions, political rallies, funerals.

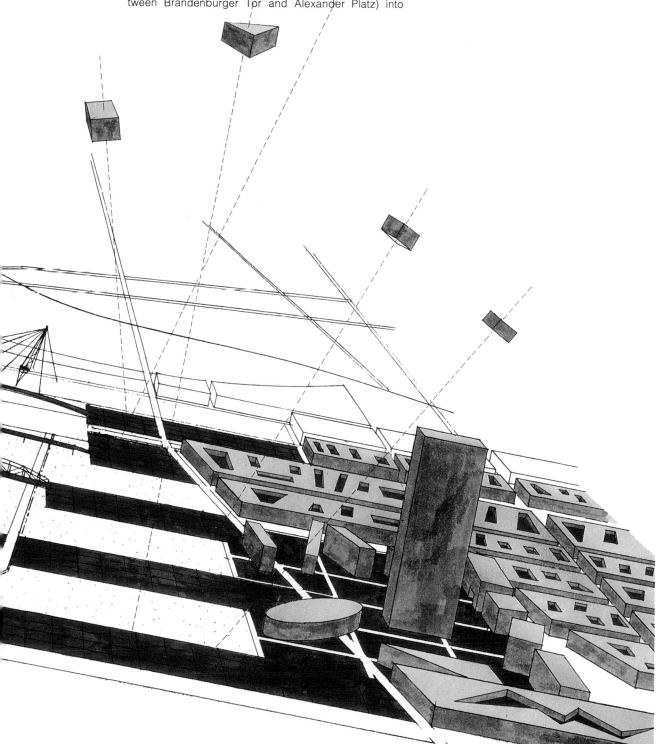

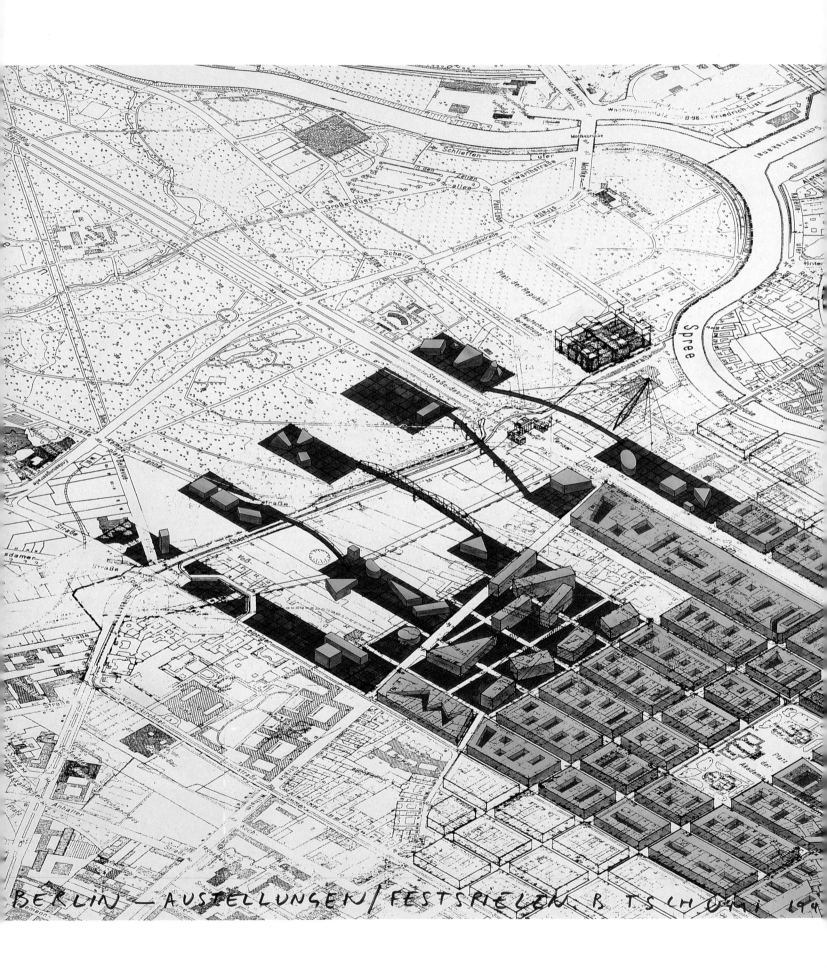

BERLIN — AUSTELLUNGEN/FESTSPIELEN B TSCHUMI 194

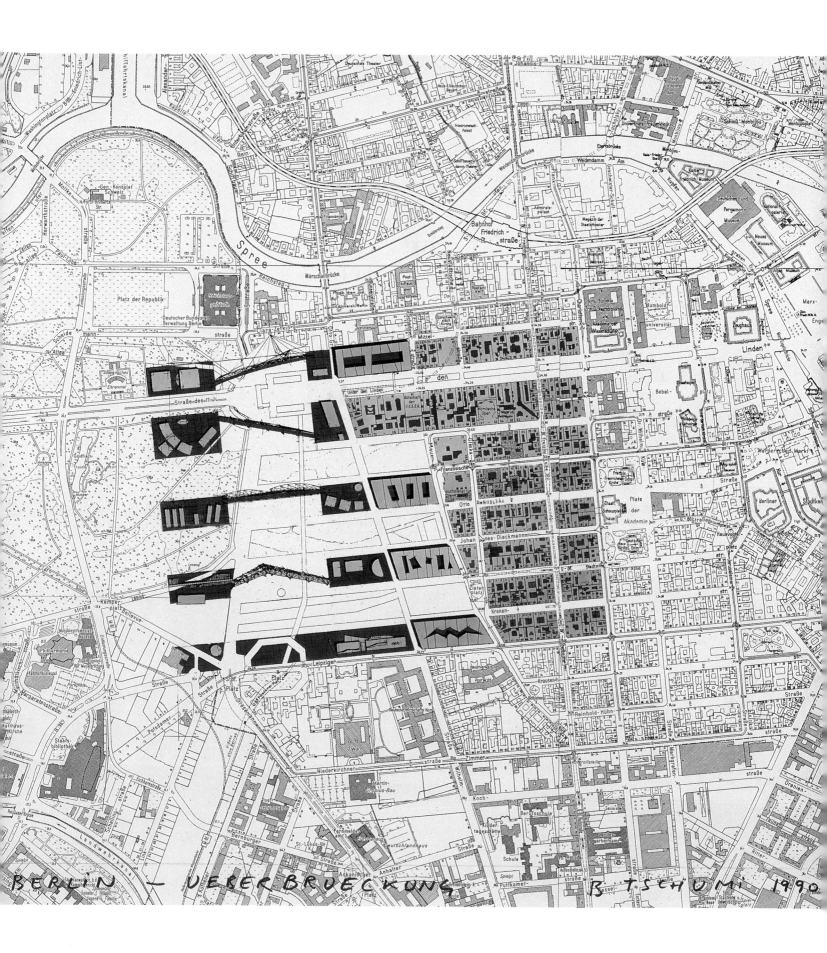

BERLIN — UEBERBRUECKUNG   B. TSCHUMI 1990

ABOVE: Axonometric of Bahnhof Friedrichstadt

OM UNGERS

URBAN ISLANDS IN A METROPOLITAN SEA

The pluralistic concept of the 'urban archipelago' – planning on historic ground.

The architectural structure of Berlin is the sum of all the ideas, thoughts, decisions, coincidences and facts of the city's history. Planned and chance events, constructive and destructive forces have determined both the city's form and its diversity. The city plan is like a textbook of events in which every mark of history is recorded. The entries read more like an enormous puzzle made up of pieces and fragments than an ordered and logical whole. From generation to generation the city has passed on an accumulation of constantly increasing and changing fragments. No generation has ever succeeded in reaching a definitive conclusion. The city has fortunately remained unfinished, discontinuous, incomplete and therefore varied and vigorous. The only continuous element is a constant dialectical process in which the thesis is refuted by the antithesis.

Any future plans for Berlin must inevitably deal with the problem of the city's history. That means developing strategies for the city's future.

Consideration should be given to whether, by selectively reducing urban pressure, or even by dismantling some parts of the present city which do not function properly, Berlin's future development might be given a unique opportunity of clearing up those areas which no longer meet required standards on architectural, social or structural grounds. At the same time, areas worth preserving should be pin-pointed and their particular characteristics either intensified or – if they are only fragmentary – complemented by further development. The enclaves thus released from urban chaos would then become 'urban islands' within the remaining, liberated urban area, creating a kind of 'urban archipelago' within a 'green lagoon of nature'.

The first step towards realising the idea of a 'city within a city' – Berlin as an 'urban archipelago' – should be the identification and selection of urban areas which possess identifiable characteristics of a quality which justifies their preservation and emphasis. These so-called 'areas of identity' should not be determined on the basis of a particular taste or on purely aesthetic grounds. Selection should be made according to the degree to which ideas and concepts exist in a pure and tangible form so that the history of the city and its architecture can be brought into line with the history of ideas.

The second step in restructuring the city in this way would be to complement the fragments which are to be preserved; this process would allow these fragments to achieve their definitive architectural and urban form. The objective needs of such fragmentary urban islands should first be identified and then dealt with individually by introducing a whole range of social facilities with a 'concentrating' function. This approach would lead to the development of complementary facilities expressly

void of bathos. In heavily developed urban areas, existing pressure should be reduced by creating open spaces such as city parks, public gardens and piazzas, whereas less heavily developed areas could be intensified by integrating centres of urban concentration.

The future architectural and design objective should consist solely in working out the intended form of each of the individual 'urban islands' selected. This would primarily involve determining, as it were, the 'physiognomy' of the area in question and shaping it so that it develops its own character. The 'urban archipelago' thus created, made up of various individual 'urban islands' of architecturally and socially distinct urban structures, would then correspond to the image of the 'city within a city'. Each district would gain its very own identity which would differ markedly from that of the other districts. Not only in this, an open urban concept in which a number of different places compete with each other, thereby increasing the diversity and complexity of the city, but also, from a political and social point of view, a pluralistic concept in which several different ideological attitudes coexist. Specifically, Märkische Viertel and Westend, Kreuzberg and Lichterfelde, and the new linear buildings in the east are all necessarily parts of a pluralistic urban concept in which the various qualities of each area complement each other, increasing the range available and consequently the freedom of choice. They are not contradictory to the point of mutual exclusion.

This pluralistic urban concept of a 'city within a city' corresponds to the current structure of an increasingly individualistic society with a wide variety of demands, wishes and expectations, in contrast to the totalitarian concept of a society in which any form of individualism is systematically repressed.

The phase of determining the actual location of the 'urban islands' would involve defining and describing the programme, as well as dealing with aspects of form and urban development. Not all new additions need necessarily be designed from scratch. It is quite conceivable that projects designed at a different time for other purposes but never realised for some reason or other might serve as models. For example, Leonidov's Palace of Culture might be taken as the model for developing the Görlitzer Bahnhof in Kreuzberg while his linear urban project for Magnetogorsk could be taken as the basis for development parallel to the 'Unter den Eichen' boulevard.

Other examples of retroactive architecture could be more specifically related to Berlin's architectural history and major past omissions could thus be redressed, for example by finally building such important projects as Mies van der Rohe's glass skyscraper at Bahnhof Friedrichstrasse to mark symbolically the entrance to the central area and as a counterpoint to the dominant East Berlin TV tower, by constructing Bruno Taut's hyperbolic dome over the Olympic stadium or by completing the chain of buildings along the Havel as envisaged by Wilhelm IV.

In their current state, both the Tiergarten area and the southern Friedrichstadt offer a unique opportunity of demonstrating the positive application of a reductionist model. All existing buildings in these areas should be painstakingly restored, irrespective of their past history, and embedded within a park. No new buildings and no new architecture would be required here, but only a park in which the present buildings would be scattered like urban palaces.

The concept of a 'city within a city' consisting of a collage of diverse urban units would be contrasted and complemented by the areas between the 'urban islands'. Some worthless urban structures should be permitted to return gradually to green areas and parkland or, as the case may be, the city should not be rebuilt there; this would certainly apply to the area around Kemperplatz. The 'urban islands' would thus be separated from each other by strips of green and nature, elucidating the metaphor of the city as a green archipelago and defining the structure of the 'city within a city'.

The green spaces create a system of modified nature and are varied in type, ranging from surburban areas to parklands, woods and urbanised agricultural use (garden allotments).

This concept would add new impetus to the polarity between nature and culture or nature and metropolis which, today, is generally absent or compromised, vaguely defined and lacking. Given the fact that such a nature/culture system would have to be designed from scratch, ie as it is of an entirely synthetic nature, it would intensify rather than reduce the metropolitan experience. After all, the metropolis is nothing other than the designation of an environment based entirely on the inventiveness of the human mind.

The green grid should also absorb the infrastructure of the modern technological age, ie in addition to an extensive road system linking the urban islands, there should be supermarkets, industrial zones and other car-dependent facilities as well as all the 20th-century typologies which are dependent on mobility rather than on location and which do not fit into a dense and properly scaled urban structure without destroying it.

In specifically applying the concept of the 'city within a city' to the existing situation, some areas would be projected more distinctly than other less significant areas because of their urban qualities. Some examples of such areas would be:
– the Kreuzberg area around Görlitzer Bahnhof
– the southern Friedrichstadt
– the central area
– the 'Spree band'
– Prenzlauer Berg
– the buildings adjacent to the Volkspark
– Müllerstrasse
– Tempelhofer Feld
– Stalinallee
– Alexanderplatz
– Museumsinsel
to name but a few particularly distinctive examples.

The areas mentioned represent widely divergent architectural structures and include block development, dissolved villa-type development, high-rises, linear building and mixed development. This diversity should be preserved and, as far as necessary, complemented by additional measures in the spirit of the existing structures. This would prevent a uniform building principle from spreading throughout the city. Individual architectural projects in line with existing urban spaces could quote historic projects which are neither intended literally nor applied in a utopic sense, but rather as an analogy to the description of urban development intentions. This could involve the following projects:
– the construction of a House of Culture in the style of Leonidov's library project on Ernst-Reuter-Platz
– the realisation of Mies van der Rohe's expressionist glass sky-scraper at Bahnhof Friedrichstrasse as a multifunctional social centre
– the realisation of Adolf Loos' design for a skyscraper for the Chicago Tribune in the form of a doric column at

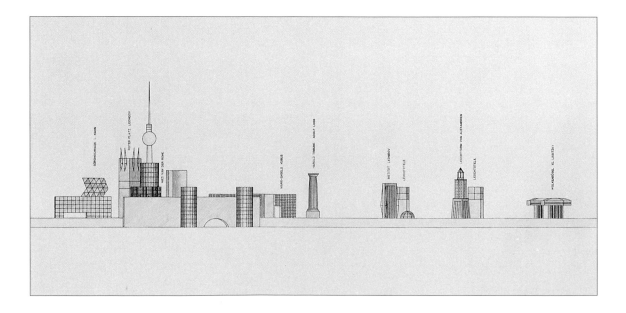

the end of the Unter den Linden boulevard.

The construction of these three historically distinctive buildings would not only give Berlin's main axis a definitive form incorporating the Brandenburger Tor and the Victory Column, but would also create a counterpoint to the prosaic dominance of the TV tower which would thus be shifted to the end of an axis reinterpreted in the light of history:

– the transposition of Leonidov's linear urban concept along the Unter den Eichen boulevard

– the transposition of New York's Central Park to the area of Görlitzer Bahnhof as a central park for Kreuzberg

– the creation of an unbroken block on the southern edge of the Volkspark along the same lines of the Royal Crescent, Bath

– the partial realisation of a linear housing projection on the banks of the Landwehrkanal along the lines of Le Corbusier's Algiers project

– the construction of cross-buildings at regular intervals along the sequence of streets known as the Generalszug as in Lissitzky's 'Cloud Props' project for Moscow

– the creation of a linear park where the Wall once ran

– the development of the Tiergarten district as an open urban landscape.

In the open spaces between the self-contained urban islands of the urban archipelago, projects of suburban quality, similar to a number of previously known proposals, should be developed, eg:

– the creation of a suburban grid according to Ludwig Hilberseimer's one-family project for Chicago

– the introduction of a regional network according to Frank Lloyd Wright's Broadacre City proposal

– the creation of mobile home parks as a substitute for inner-city living and as an alternative for country living and leisure-oriented living

– the creation of sport and leisure facilities, from parks and playgrounds to game preserves and artificial landscapes for Alpine sports as well as leisure landscapes in Walt Disney style, but also with natural landscapes and nature parks

– the creation of industrial parks à la Silicon Valley with leisure facilities such as play areas, bathing and sport facilities for the workforce.

From an historical point of view, the 'city within a city' model transforms Wilhelm IV's architectural concept of 'architectonic incidents' for the Havel into fragments of historic memory. In his historic design, a system of architectural monuments reflecting history was superimposed on the Havel landscape between Potsdam and Berlin, transforming it into a cultural landscape in the humanistic sense. In this plan, memory becomes reality and reality becomes the experience of history.

It is a landscape in which the individual aspects of various cultural areas, ideas and theses are placed in relation to each other. This antithetical world of architectural styles and references includes the Pfaueninsel with its Baroque castle ruins and dairy embodying a romantic world of the past, the Gatow church by Stüler which exudes the rational spirit of the Italian Renaissance, Pfingstberg with its antique temple fragments, Sacrow church in the Byzantine style, Schinkel's casino as a document of the Enlightenment and a Classicistic ideal and, of course, Glienicke with its Neo-Gothic Babelsberg and Stüler's pump-unit. With the architectural islands, the city itself becomes transformed into an archipelago of special places. The objects gain their context solely through memory and an awareness of history. Similarly, the structure of the Havel landscape holds the key to the concept of Berlin as a 'city within a city', as an 'urban archipelago' which embraces Berlin's humanistic tradition, transposing it in modified form to the present day.

These are just a few of the topics whose significance should be discussed in relation to the city's future. The problem to be discussed – and this applies particularly to Berlin – is not one of designing a completely new environment, but of complementing and transforming what already exists; not of inventing a new urban system, but of improving the existing one; not of starting anew, but of continuity. Not of striving for a new utopia, but of designing a better reality; not of designing another world, but of improving the existing one: the future of Berlin lies in the interaction of heterogeneous parts.

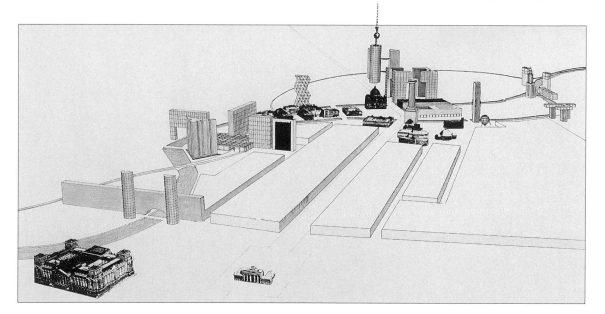

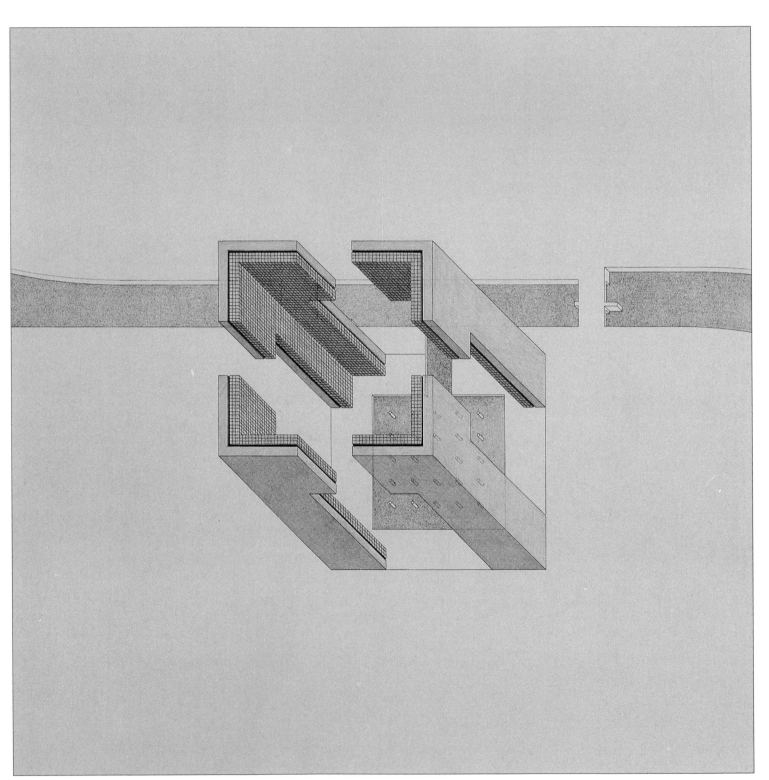

ABOVE: Axonometric of Marx-Engels Kubus